MY DESERT BLOG CABIN

How I Designed And Constructed My Desert Home

Cat Cohen

Published by Cat Cohen Unltd
ROAD HORIZONS DIVISION

OTHER BOOKS by CAT COHEN

Road Horizons Division
CAT TRACKS – A Budget Train Travel Adventure (2018)
A frugal, insightful, and visual journey across the U.S. by train from the colorful desert southwest to the historic coastal northeast with stops in Albuquerque, Chicago, Buffalo, Albany, Gloucester, Providence, Peekskill, New York City, and points in between.

ROAD POEMS U.S.A. – Poetry And Photographs From The Highways And Byways Of America (2010/2018)
Over 130 down-to-earth poems and 90 unique colorful photo images from the author's coast-to-coast journeys through 25 Southwestern, Northwestern, Midwestern, Southeastern, and Northeastern states.

TALES OF A CENSUS WORKER (2011)
A journal of the author's experiences while canvassing small town citizens, horse ranchers, fearful Hispanics, and anti-government holdouts for the 2010 census in the Southern California high desert.

ROAD STORIES SOUTHWEST (2010/2013)
Way-off-the-beaten-path travel adventures from three journeys in New Mexico, Arizona, Southern Colorado, and Northeastern Baja California.

THE LONGER ROAD HOME (2015)
An inspiring novel of recovery narrated by Sam Freberg, a bohemian Jewish musician born into a dysfunctional LA family in the 1940s, his struggle for self-acceptance as a gay man, and how he combats and survives addictions and an AIDS diagnosis.

Savory Publications Division
DIVING OUT IN LA (1984/1986)
co-author Avry Budka   A nostalgic and witty guide to the best low-cost eateries in the Greater Los Angeles area during the 1980s.   Rave reviewed in the LA Times and several local periodicals, it became a cult classic before the advent of the Food Network

CHICKEN SOUPS FROM AROUND THE WORLD (2011)
Chicken soup recipes from 13 states and 39 countries covering techniques and ingredients from equatorial Africa to arctic Alaska and all temperate zones in between.   This cookbook is designed for traditional old-fashioned take-your-time as well as modern quick throw-together styles of cooking,

WHINE CONNOISSEUR'S GUIDE (2009)
co-author Avry Budka   A tongue firmly placed-in-cheek guidebook to the history of whines, the whinemaker's art, whine categories, regional whines, popular whineries, whining and dining, whines for every occasion, and whiner's entertainment.

Koan Music Division
SONGWRITING FOR YOUR ORIGINAL ACT (2006/2012)
A motivating, informative guidebook that asks songwriters important questions about themselves as an original act. The answers help define one's performance, message, audience, genre, style, and industry format.

MY DESERT BLOG CABIN

by Cat Cohen

Edited by Avry Budka and Karen Robinson-Stark

Photographs by Cat Cohen
Additional photographs by Joseph Varga and George Miller

C 2009/2018 David Cat Cohen

ISBN # 978-0-9899390-7-2

Printed in the United States of America

Published by Cat Cohen Unltd
Road Horizons Division
PO Box 275
Morongo Valley, CA 92256

cat@catcohen.com
www.catcohen.com

First edition - October, 2009
Second edition - July, 2018

Muses no more what ere ye be
In fancy pleasures roam
But sing by truth inspired with me
The pleasures of a home

John Clare

ACKNOWLEDGMENTS

I'd like to thank my good friend and editress, (my own contribution to our ever-evolving lexicon) **Avry Budka,** for her support and tasteful reworking of the early drafts of this book. Besides helping me articulate this story with much more clarity, she gave me objective feedback when my descriptions became so personal that it was obvious I got lost in a world of my own. Another very good friend, **Karen Robinson-Stark,** gave me invaluable writing input and critiques, especially in he first chapter on my formative years.

I also want to express my deep gratitude for the great craftsmanship and invaluable advice of my neighbor, **Jeff Kern,** who became my contractor for the building of this house. Without Jeff's assistance this home would never have become as functional, efficient and as beautiful as it turned out to be. My Morongo Basin construction crew, which included **Sean Short, Blaine Ross**, **Andrew Griffin, Clarence Chambers** and **Art Rios,** were very helpful and professional in their contributions to my dream house.

In addition I would like to mention the support and labor of several friends who saw me through this long ordeal: **Ruth Ellen Billion, George Miller, Randy Budka** and **Joe Varga**. Not only did they lend a hand when work needed to be done, they each in their own way were there to help me celebrate and/or commiserate as situations came and went. Another friend, **Stina Jacobson,** was also a helpful sounding board through all my construction adventures, and her son **Gus Jacobson** was welcome company when I began setting up my cabin.

TABLE OF CONTENTS

Part 1 – IN THE BEGINNING………

Part 2 - MORONGO BASIN - HO!

Part 3 - CABIN FEVER

Part 4 - TEMP TO PERM MAKEOVER
Plan A - Adding 3 Rooms

Part 6 - THE FOLLOWING YEAR

The Props assist the House until the House is built
And then the Props withdraw and adequate, erect,
The House supports itself and ceases to recollect
The Augur and the Carpenter – just such a retrospect
Hath the perfected Life – a past of plank and nail
And slowness – then the scaffolds drop affirming it a Soul

Emily Dickinson

INTRODUCTION

My Desert Blog Cabin is the product of two years of blogging about how I designed and built my home in Morongo Valley, a small rural settlement in the high desert twenty miles north of Palm Springs. It is both a description of the construction process and its effect on me. Not only did I need to let go of my urban preferences and prejudices, I had to acquire a new set of tools for living. I discovered depths of self-reliance as I coped with the elements in a more extreme climate and an environment. As I built my "little house on the desert prairie" I was schooled in finding and purchasing real estate, designing residential space, participating in and surviving residential construction, handling government bureaucracy, wading through the inconsistent world of home improvement centers, and distinguishing important differences between manufactured and stick-built homes. Since my career in music had not provided any training in these pursuits, I had a lot to learn.

I've called the shots as I experienced them. Get ready to read a "build and tell" book. When people, stores and institutions were good to me, I praise their efforts and contributions. Likewise, when I encountered anyone unscrupulous, selfish, petty, or incompetent, I pull no punches in describing their shortcomings. Although personifying many of these heroes and villains in detail, I've left out their names to protect both the innocent and the guilty. During this challenging time, I met all kinds of people, maybe not as sophisticated as my urban neighbors had been, but gifted with great practical common sense. The unaffected warmth and helpfulness of my new desert community has made a lasting contribution to my life.

I hope you find my story a useful tale, benefiting equally from my accomplishments and my mistakes. If you ever decide to build like I did, I wish you all the fun that I had and a lot less of the headaches. If you just want to accompany me on my journey from ethnic city slicker to down home desert dweller, welcome aboard.

Cat Cohen

PART 1 – AS THE TWIG WAS BENT
Native Born Angeleno

The Jews may have wandered in the desert for 40 years before finding the promised land, but in my case it was the reverse. It took this boy more than 40 years of wandering in the urban jungle before I found that my promised land actually was in the desert. I grew up in Los Angeles in a working class Jewish family (i.e. no doctors, no lawyers, etc.). Most of my childhood was spent in small apartments and modest homes in various neighborhoods of this sprawling metropolis. I was born at St. Vincent's, a Catholic hospital on the corner of 3rd Street and Alvarado, where the doctor predicted that I would grow up to be a swimmer and have broad shoulders. Obviously not a psychic, he probably told that to all the mothers that delivered boys in the maternity ward.

My parents took me home to their one-room apartment where I spent the first two years of my life. When I was older, they told me that they were so poor at that time they didn't even have a refrigerator, only an icebox. If this venerable residence were still standing today, it would be a stone's throw from LA's Convention Center. The building was razed many years ago to make room for the nexus of the Harbor (110) and Santa Monica (10) freeways. I have passed by its ghost thousands of times in my daily commutes.

By the time I was two, my folks were able to rent a tiny house just northwest of Venice Boulevard and La Brea Avenue, a neighborhood that is predominantly Afro-American now. My earliest memories are of that house. I remember the wood-framed structure itself, a large lemon tree in the back yard, and my mom walking me the half-block to the Venice Boulevard Red Line streetcar for rides with her downtown and occasionally to the beach. We rode the original light rail, not the sadly diminished version LA has today.

I was fortunate to be the first child and experience the earlier, happier days of my parents' soon-to-be acrimonious marriage. My sisters never had that secure beginning. There was an inverse relationship between our family's emotional well-being and our state of prosperity. The harmony between my parents decreased as my father's income increased. As his small business making inexpensive radios grew into the responsibilities of manufacturing stereos on a larger scale, so did the distance grow between my dad and our family. Our home life reminds me of Orson Wells' portrayal of Hearst in the movie *Citizen Kane*. The dining room table got longer as the communication became less and less, then fell to almost nothing.

By the early 1950s, my two younger sisters had been born. The family moved to a larger apartment in a new complex in North Hollywood, which is where I attended elementary school. We had a second story flat in such a drab gray non-descript row of buildings that I hardly remember it. One thing that stands out for me from that time was the large laundry room full of washers and dryers. My mom would have me wait there, then run up to tell her when the wash was done. I would spend hours fascinated by the sounds and sights of all those whirring machines spinning around and around (a precursor to my future obsessive-compulsive personality).

A couple of years later we moved into Hollywood to a two-bedroom apartment. We lived next to where the 101 freeway was being constructed. I remember playing in the construction zone where I had an unfortunate accident falling on some boards and driving a nail through my hand. The ride to the emergency room and the nurses dressing my wounds afterwards still remain vivid images.

A more pleasant event happened in second grade. I was one of the lucky kids from my class to appear on the TV show "Art Linkletter's House Party". I wore a big bow tie for the occasion and acted like a real ham for the cameras (seeds of the theatrical side of my nature).

When I was seven, my parents decided we children should learn about our ethnic heritage. So we moved this time to the Jewish neighborhood near Fairfax Avenue. My father's growing business enabled us to purchase a 3-bedroom Spanish-style house on a side street just west of the main drag with a tiny yard in the back. I strongly recall its dark green exterior and the dark brown, wood-framed porch that gave it a hacienda look. These colors perfectly matched the dark emotions that often erupted inside this residence.

Our small backyard housed a huge avocado tree that provided a bumper crop of fruit each year. It was so prolific we shipped numerous cartons of avocados to our thrilled New York relatives, and sold quite a few to some local produce stores. Behind the enormous tree was a cement incinerator where we burned our weekly trash. A couple of years later, the city banned this practice to combat smog in the LA basin. Keeping the original Red Line instead of building so many freeways might have been a better idea.

As far as the Jewishness of the area, there was no mistaking it. Yiddish culture was everywhere. Most of our neighbors were orthodox; two of them were rabbis. Our family was not the slightest bit religious. Ironically, my secular parents had a fondness for serving bacon for breakfast. Keeping kosher was as foreign to us as to any white bread and mayonnaise *Leave It to Beaver* family. My father not only did not believe in God, the ironclad way he ruled the family made it seem that he considered himself to be the almighty.

We were so non-observant, that one Yom Kippur, a day when many Jews fast and atone for their sins, my sisters and I unwittingly cooked up a half pound of bacon. When my parents smelled the odors wafting outside, they were so ashamed; they made sure we went out of town on all future high holidays.

One of the Jewish traditions that I did learn in this neighborhood was how to shop for bargains. At a young age I managed to deal with the local shopkeepers' chicanery. My mom would send me out to a nearby bakery with just enough money for a half-pound of marble cake. Invariably, the woman behind the counter would slice off two thirds of a pound and try to charge me more for it. Since I didn't have enough money for more than half a pound, I usually got the larger amount for the lesser price because she couldn't put it back. Later, I'd pretend I only had enough money for less even when I had more in my pocket. A shrewd shopper was born in the 'hood.

My parents' bickering and frustration with each other increasingly dominated our family life. As their arguments grew into full-scale rages, I would retreat into fantasies of travel and escape. I often rode my bicycle to visit travel agencies to collect brochures for phantom trips to Europe and other far-away places. I'd pedal ten, twenty miles or more, bringing back countless descriptions and photos of possible trips and itineraries. I planned many ideal seven-countries-in-seventeen-days tours. After a while, I had amassed so many brochures, I almost could have opened up my own agency.

Yet, during this period, there were a few times when the family shared some genuine togetherness and happiness. We would pile into the family Buick and drive to some inexpensive location such as Bakersfield or Desert Hot Springs. Our destination was usually a cheap motel with a large pool and some low-priced restaurants nearby. For us there never were any Hiltons, bellboys, valet parking, gourmet dinners, ritzy shopping arcades, or amusement parks, and few tourist stops. Just the same, they were a welcome change of pace and made for some happy memories (the basis of my knack for having a good time within economic restraints).

After several years in the Fairfax district, my parents decided to seek a larger house, for a budget price, in the San Fernando Valley. After much house hunting, they settled on a large, sterile, cheaply-built, brand new tract house in Northridge. It was constructed on a half-acre of denuded land, raped and pillaged of its lovely orange trees and rich topsoil. This sprawling suburban home had many large rooms, huge front and back yards, and walls as thin as pastry shells. You could hear a person sneeze three rooms away. We kids were subject to every volatile family discussion and relentless argument.

The couple of years we resided in this oversized cracker-box of a home were far from pleasant. Though a few of the neighbors were nice down-to-earth people, many of them had the kind of pretentious personalities that matched the inexpensive self-importance of these huge tract houses masquerading as fine homes. An air of competition hid an underlying insecurity and chronic threat of impending implosion. The karmic outcome of these negative emotions expressed itself many years later when the Northridge earthquake of 1995 struck the area. Several of these residences, including ours, were red-tagged (uninhabitable, pending serious repair) after that devastating event.

It wasn't long before my parents realized their mistake and moved us to a smaller, less impressive, but more solidly built home nearby. By this time, I was preparing to go to college to get a degree in music. Soon, I was accepted at UCLA, some 25 miles away. After commuting for the first year, I pleaded with my parents to let me live on campus. Because I'd already started to make money by giving piano lessons, they agreed that, if I paid for my own books and tuition, they'd finance my dorm expenses. This was a deal I did not refuse.

In college, I studied music with passion and abandon. I made many new friends with varied backgrounds and interests, falling in with a crowd that kindled an interest in hiking and camping. Although I had no previous camping experience, when two of my high school buddies invited me to join them on a three-week camping trip to Colorado, I jumped at the chance.

Looking back on this adventure, what I remember most is freezing my butt sleeping in the snow near Lake Tahoe; cooking up cans of chili and beef stew in a Gunnison, Colorado campground; sleeping in my friend's station wagon during an unbelievable rainstorm; and driving through southwest Colorado's awesome San Juan Mountains. By the time we returned home, I was a dyed-in-the-wool camper.

That trip was a life-changing experience. My love for nature and my willingness to give up life's comforts to be close to it became a high priority. My heart and soul have traveled the highways and byways leading me away from my native birthplace ever since.

Travel Lodges & Sweat Lodges

For many years after graduating from university life, I made a modest living as a music teacher, songwriter and musician. My frugal upbringing had prepared me to deal with an uncertain income and a minimalist life style. I took vacations on the cheap, staying mostly in budget motels. Better yet, I'd spend nights sleeping under the stars in campgrounds or nestled safely in one of my various and sundry vehicles.

In my twenties, my friends and I would fantasize about buying rural acreage. To my knowledge, even though we each eventually bought city houses and settled down, none of us had acted on this desire. As I reached my fifties, I still carried within me this unrealized dream. I had observed that urbanites like us always managed to wind up using our disposable income for other things.

In the meantime, I developed an interest in spiritual study. This led me to yoga, meditation, and Native American ceremonies. My first encounter with a sweat lodge was on a New Age weekend of multi-cultural rituals that included Hindu mantra, Hawaiian massage, Buddhist chanting, and culminated in what I'd describe as a gringo sweat.

This whetted my appetite for the real thing. I started seeking out people that practiced sweats. Eventually I found a group that met a few times a year in the high desert near Victorville. We'd build a lodge out of branches, twigs and blankets, light a huge fire to heat rocks, and have a Lakota Sioux medicine man we knew pour water on these heated lava stones and lead us in traditional prayer. We'd all sing Lakota songs to the ancestors and four directions. Ceremonial drums and Indian flute music often accompanied these observances. A communal potluck feast usually followed.

The Good Earth & The Spirit Sings

My interest in spending time in natural spaces grew. So did my love for the desert itself. An experience that helped move these desires into action was reading a novel by Pearl Buck. *The Good Earth* is an in-depth look into Chinese culture though the story of a multi-generational family. The main character's rise, fall and redemption touched me deeply. After gaining and losing so much in his life, he retained ownership of many acres of land, and his love for it comforted him greatly in his later years. Since my urban family had no history of rural land ownership, he became a role model. A cousin of mine on the east coast became another example to follow when she and her husband purchased a country home on a large parcel in upstate New York. After a visit there, her place was such a welcome change from city life, I wanted to experience this for myself.

Two events contributed to making this possible. When my dad died in the mid-80s, he left me enough of an inheritance to purchase a small home of my own in Los Angeles. By the time Y2K arrived, its equity had risen to where I had potential to draw from it. The other factor was that after several years of having accumulated credit card debt, I had paid most of it off. My credit rating now qualified me for a home equity loan. However, I brushed aside the prospect of buying some acreage. Me, a landowner?   Only in my dreams.

Then, one weekend in early 2001, when I was car camping in the desert north of Palm Springs, I happened to bring along a CD of Native American flute music by Carlos Nakai. The recording brought back memories of the sweat lodges I'd once attended. That night I dreamed of walking on land that I owned. I awoke to find that I had camped underneath a real estate sign that advertised land for sale. Feeling that this was more than a coincidence, I called the agent's phone number and left a message.

He returned my call a few days later. This particular property had 25 acres and a mobile home for sale for $125,000, well out of my price range. When the agent asked what I was looking for, I mentioned my desire to buy some land. Perhaps I might build on it later for my retirement. He suggested I'd find smaller, cheaper parcels over the hill going up the grade on Highway 62 in the Morongo Basin. The communities of Morongo Valley, Yucca Valley, Joshua Tree and beyond were fairly unknown to me. Little did I know that this area would turn out to play such a significant role in my future.

PART 2 - MORONGO BASIN - HO!
One Log Cabin Too Late

Driving home smitten with the idea of owning my own piece of the rock, I could hardly wait to begin the search. For generations, my ancestors had essentially been living in densely populated communities whether it was LA or New York City here in the U.S., Warsaw in Poland, or Krakow, a large city in what had been Austria-Hungary. By purchasing some land, I'd be breaking this tradition, something I was eager to do. Though my immigrant grandparents each had been totally ethno-centric, my father was a member of the second generation of Jews wanting to blend into American society. I took this urge to live the American experience further than he did. I was led to an area where I'd essentially be a fish out of water, one of the few non-Christians, and, as I was to find out later, one of the few politically non-conservatives as well.

Back in LA, I went on the internet to check out real estate listings in the Morongo Basin to see if the agent knew what he was talking about. He did. There were many two to five acre parcels in my price range (under $25,000), some even with small cabins. Until then, the prospect of a weekend getaway hadn't occurred to me. I printed out a list of possibilities and could hardly wait to see them for myself.

A couple of weekends later I drove the 120 miles to this potential new sanctuary. The first community up the grade was Morongo Valley. I'd been through this locality before, but thought of it only as a hamlet one passes on the road to Joshua Tree National Park and the more scenic alternate route to Needles and Las Vegas. At 2,700 feet in elevation, this area is noticeably cooler and greener than the desert down below. In researching the region I learned that it is part of the large Mojave Desert, while Palm Springs and Desert Hot Springs are considered to be Sonoran Desert, a contrast in flora and fauna. This upper region is in San Bernardino County, while the lower area is part of Riverside County.

Charming and rustic, Morongo Valley housed a few dingy businesses and dusty houses down dirt roads on large parcels of land zoned RL for rural living, euphemistically in the trade called horse property. Corrals were common here, something that appealed to the animal lover in me. It was good that I didn't have my departed Jewish mother along. She had enough problems with the funky apartments that I'd lived in near Venice Beach when I was in my twenties. These tumbledown shacks would have given her the willies.

The first listing took me down three difficult to navigate dirt roads. But the ad's description of a log cabin on five acres of land had filled me with fantasy images of wild-west living. The price was $20,000, well within my budget. When I first set my eyes on this old cabin from a distance, my heart melted. Every "little house on the prairie" movie I'd ever seen played in mind. Set well apart from any neighbors, it even had its own electric pole and meter. I thought I was having beginner's luck. My heart dropped when I read a sign with the words "sale pending". A call to the agent confirmed this. So much for my good fortune. I found out later the cabin was decayed and rat infested, that the buyer had to raze it and build a whole new structure. Perhaps my luck wasn't as bad as I had thought. I could hear my mom breathing a huge sigh of relief.

Yucca Valley, Joshua Tree, Twentynine Palms, Wonder Valley & Pioneertown

Having seen this possibility, I no longer searched for acreage alone. I now had my sights set on a getaway residence as well. At that time, no other listings with structures were available in Morongo Valley. I needed to travel farther into the desert to find one.

I drove up another grade to the redneck suburban town of Yucca Valley. This unremarkable city of 25,000 inhabitants has a main drag lined with miles of non-descript strip malls. It is strongly influenced by the marine base near Twentynine Palms. Young men with crew cuts in army fatigues are commonplace. There are also numerous Christian churches. This military-meets-Bible-Belt culture gives the town a strong Southern and Middle-American feel. The only business that was open after 9pm was the local WalMart. The eateries then were also boring, biscuits 'n gravy being the best item the city had to offer. Much has changed in the past few years as enterprises like Starbuck's and Applebee's have opened their doors. Even with these culinary improvements, nothing would have passed muster (or should I say mustard) with my parents had they been able to visit me here. Not a single pastrami sandwich or even decent dill pickle could be found within the city limits.

The next listing in my price range was just north of Yucca Valley in Yucca Mesa, a sparse, flat uninteresting area. This plain 1-bedroom pink stucco house was as unromantic as the log cabin was a heartthrob. At $25,000, it was in need of major rehab and serious trash removal. Even imagining the parcel cleaned up and redone, the view left a lot to be desired. I didn't need to hear the word "feh" from any of my relatives. This place would be the kind of getaway even I could hardly wait to get away from.

Next were a couple of similar mismatches in Landers, a community made famous by a large earthquake in the early 90s. A bit north of Yucca Mesa, Lander's desolate landscape and remoteness did not appeal to me, even though there were many affordable properties available. Many of these buildings were rundown shacks with peeling paint and loose boards banging in the wind. They could be fixed up, but I couldn't see myself staying that far out in the desert.

I drove back down to Highway 62 and headed east to the small town of Joshua Tree, the gateway to Joshua Tree National Park. Its few blocks of dusty businesses had more character than Yucca Valley or Landers. North of the highway there were a few blocks of inexpensive homes on tiny city lots with water and utilities. Though in my price range, they were not to my liking. There was little style, view, space or privacy.

Continuing to the next city of Twentynine Palms, I encountered much the same thing. This larger town has some interesting shops and many colorful murals. Once again, there were no cabins in my price range, only small houses on tiny lots surrounded by many others. The strong military presence here was not my idea of ambience. Neither my father nor I ever served in the military, but I did do a stint in the Peace Corps. This would never have scored points for me with the locals. In addition, its distance was a drawback.

The adjoining community of Wonder Valley contains no businesses, mostly cheap cabins spaced far apart on large lots. The great views of the western areas of the Morongo Basin are absent. Many properties were in disarray, and it seemed the rumors I'd heard about meth labs might be true. I was put off by the potential danger. The longer commute from LA was a definite minus. I'm not surprised that quite a few rock musicians have recently bought places here. When I used to play in rock bands in my younger years, drugs and edge came with the territory. The FBI did an investigation on me before I entered the Peace Corps. Somehow, they decided I was OK. Today, if I were to live in Wonder Valley, Homeland Security might be out there in full force. This edgy place was not for me.

Heading back west, I made a stop in Pioneertown, an old western movie locale with horses, stables and a great country music biker bar, Pappy and Harriet's. I'd visited the area previously and was attracted to its colorful character. In summer, on the central thoroughfare, Mane Street, locals stage mock gunfights for visitors. At 4,000 feet in elevation, the vegetation is lush with numerous Joshua trees, junipers and pinon pines. Large boulders dot the landscape. Its proximity to snow-capped mountains makes the area picturesque. Many cowboy films have been shot here. There were a few fairly pricy one-acre parcels for sale in the area, but no cabins were on the market. As much as the place appealed to my inner cowboy, to build here would have been beyond my budget.

The trip was disappointing, but on my next visit I hoped to do better. A following junket led me to a few potential properties in Yucca Valley. Its paved streets, electricity, municipal water, and trash pickup may fit the middle-of-the-road buyer, but did not ring my bells. Being close enough to neighbors to hear their televisions and stereos negated my reason for buying a place out of LA. In the mid-90s, a two-bedroom house on a city lot here sold for $40,000. By 2001, the price had doubled. I had neither interest nor funds for a home here. I did find a small, fixer-upper house with large trees and some charm for $25,000. By the time I inquired, someone had snapped it up.

Goodbye Cabin, Hello Land

It seemed that my chances of obtaining land with a building on it were slim to none. The 400 square foot homestead cabin had become a thing of the past, unless I wanted to go very deep into the desert. I didn't. If I was going to give up buying a structure of my own, I wanted a parcel closer to LA. Morongo Valley and western Yucca Valley had views of snow-capped mountains and pine trees. They were nearer to Palm Springs and the mineral spas of Desert Hot Springs. So I returned to my original game plan and began looking for some land closer in on which I could eventually build.

Making appointments with local real estate agents, I soon discovered that buying land can be as tricky as purchasing a residence. Besides size, location and price, one has to consider its access to utilities and vehicles. Some parcels are on paved roads, some on dirt roads, and some need 4-wheel drives to get there. I was shown reasonably priced acreages in West Yucca with great views that were difficult to access. They were so far from utilities it would cost a small fortune to get connected to them. One day I was taken to an amazing view lot on a hilltop in the area with a pad ready for a house to be constructed on it. It had a three-hundred-and-sixty-degree vista of the mountain and desert region. The main problem was that it took a strenuous hike to walk up there and required a sturdy jeep with oversized wheels to ascend its steep grade to park in front. It wasn't doable.

Tiny View Lot With A Crazy Neighbor

On one excursion, I found a small lot with God's gift of a view on a steep hillside in West Yucca right next to a paved road. I couldn't believe its price was only $5,500. This appealed to my frugality, and I immediately started drawing up construction plans in my mind. Though it was on the edge of a cliff, the first house that I bought in LA was built on stilts into the bedrock on a similar site. Perhaps I could do the same here. Though some problems come along with a perch, they were balanced by its view and privacy. The parcel was still on the market. I now had a real contender to consider.

On my second visit I found the lot just as appealing with its sweeping vista overlooking both San Jacinto and San Gorgonio peaks. A negative was an area at the end of the road where a layer of trash indicated that riff-raff congregated there. Seduced by the view and the price, I put my blinders on and decided I'd somehow deal with this potential liability.

I began the first of my prospective property sleepovers, parking in front of a site, staying in my car overnight. Despite my qualms about strange characters in the area, none appeared. I fell asleep dreaming of a new house on stilts. However, at 3 A.M. a man yelling at the top of his lungs awakened me. This disturbance came from the second story balcony of a large house across the street. Since I was the only other person around, I had no idea if he was cursing at me, or he was nuts. In either case, this was not a good omen. It reinforced my initial bad vibe.

Deterred, but not totally discouraged, the next day I stopped at the local Building and Safety office to inquire about the lot. It had setback requirements and was in an earthquake fault zone. I knew there were reasons for its cheap price tag. The setback I could deal with. This would mean a larger front yard, more deck areas in the back, and longer stilts. Since this whole area is earthquake prone, its zoning was no surprise. But now I was filled with foreboding.

When I returned home, that night in my sleep I kept hearing the screams of the crazy man on his balcony. Twisting and turning, I woke up with the realization that, as much as I loved the view and the price, this place was not a fit. Land is more complicated than a slice of marble cake. Even though my father might have had tears roll down his cheeks at the thought of a great deal that got away, I had to part company with him. I sensed correctly that a bargain filled with misery is no bargain at all.

Desert Theater Outpost

Discouraged, I gave parcel hunting a rest. Occasionally I'd look for new listings, but they were few and far between. A few weeks later, a prospect took me to a new realtor. I wasn't thrilled about his talkative personality, but he had some good leads. He showed me a lot on a quiet road in Morongo Valley for the reasonable price of $6,500. It was not as large as I was looking for, only an acre and a quarter, but the setting was appealing with yucca trees and cactuses. Plus it was situated on a block of quaint older ranch houses.

Next door was a rustic dwelling with fenced in horses and goats. Across the street was a small theater in the middle of nowhere. The marquee announced a current showing of a two-woman play. Having written some plays and musicals myself, I was tickled at the opportunity to be close to a possible outlet for my creativity. When the agent said the owner of the parcel was Native American, with my affinity for Indians, I found the coincidence too strong to ignore.

I went home that night with new visions in my head. The view was nothing to write home about, yet the place seemed peaceful with a semblance of culture nearby. It was worth a sleepover. I revisited the lot and slept peacefully in front, waking to the sounds of farm animals and roosters crowing nearby. No balcony expletives disturbed me. A few neighbors whom I spoke to were very welcoming. The only negative I could foresee was the need to grade the parcel and clear some of its profuse vegetation.

I called the agent and made an offer for $5,500. He replied that the price was firm. Bakery haggling be damned, I really wanted the place, and offered the full amount. When he had my good faith deposit of $1,000 in hand, he said we'd be in escrow very soon. I had to endure his long personal narratives in order to discuss any business, and this narcissistic chatter grated on my nerves. When I could break through his narrations, he said the papers were almost ready to sign but there were delays on the seller's end.

Meanwhile, I thought about a future house I could construct on the lot. Since building from the ground up was expensive, I researched manufactured homes. Online, I learned these started at $30,000. With site and preparation charges, set-up and delivery fees, school board taxes, permits and a few other costs, this was out of my reach at the time. For the present, I could level out an area to park my vehicle and sleep on my land. At least I'd have a beachhead on my future. I was going to be a happy camper, or so I thought.

My One-Act Play Closes

The reference to the best-laid plans of mice and men in this case was right. My offer was provisionally accepted, but we still weren't in escrow. I waited patiently, then increasingly impatiently. As weeks passed, I learned the seller was infirm, lived a distance away, had no telephone, and all negotiations had to go through a conservator. Each new delay gave my agent another opportunity to talk about his sick relatives, marital troubles, and whatever else he felt like venting. I was not at all pleased.

Additional time was lost when the conservator was fired and a new one took over. After two more months and no progress, I wanted out of the deal. Just when I thought I could take no more, the agent called to say that there were further complications. Three other relatives on the trust deed turned out to be deceased. This meant the transaction would have to go through probate and additional months of court processing. At this point, the agent and I both wanted out. Though relieved to get my deposit back, I was so disappointed I felt like abandoning my pursuit of land altogether. A couple of weeks later, the September 11th terrorist attacks occurred. This sudden change in the international landscape only added to my disillusion.

Something there is that doesn't love a wall,
That sends the frozen-ground-swell under it,
And spills the upper boulders in the sun;
And makes gaps even two can pass abreast.

Before I built a wall I'd ask to know
What I was walling in or walling out,
And to whom I was like to give offence.
Something there is that doesn't love a wall.

Robert Frost

PART 3 - CABIN FEVER
Little House On The Bluff

During the disturbing aftermath of September 11, looking for land dropped off my radar. After time began to heal my wounds, out of curiosity I took a casual peek at the internet real estate listings. I wasn't eager to resume the search, but a weekend retreat still appealed to me. I had a feeling that some people worried about the state of political and economic insecurity at that time might be selling their properties. I was right. There were several new listings on the market, and the prices were going down, not up.

I came upon an item that caught my attention. a non-descript rectangular building, not at all romantic or impressive. But it was a cabin (YES!). And it was in Morongo Valley (YES, YES!). It was on 2 1/2 acres of land (YES, YES, YES!) And the seller was asking only $17,000 (MY GOD, YES!). I read on. There had to be a catch. There were no utilities - no water, no gas, and no electricity. But at that price, at least I'd have a place where I could camp out.

Sensing that I could buy an investment property for the future and something to use right away, I called the agent and got the address. The following Saturday I drove to the structure, having to navigate a mile of dirt roads to reach the site. Unlike internet dating, the cabin was true to its online photo, a boring box. What the picture didn't capture was its awesome view. Situated on a bluff just above a large dry wash, the cabin faced a panoramic valley vista with an array of snow-capped mountains in the distance. San Gorgonio, in all its splendor, towered above in the distance. This majestic peak would have brought my Chinese hero in The Good Earth great comfort.

The land immediately around the cabin had been graded into large flat zones with hardly any brush. In contrast, the wash below was full of large graceful desert willows and many creosote bushes and cholla cactuses. This was far from an expanse of lawns and golf courses, but not sterile desert either. I was looking for nature and privacy, and this place had both. If I would have travel a ways to satisfy ethnic food cravings, so be it. The covered wagon pioneers survived without sending out for restaurant delivery. So could I.

I tried to peek inside the cabin, but its windows were boarded up. The fanlight glass on the only door let in so little light, that even when I jumped up to look through it, I could see nothing within. Nevertheless, I called the agent to say I was interested, and we made a date to view it. I was on pins and needles all week. The place had the location I wanted, a great view, and it was affordable. I hoped the cabin would be OK without rats and snakes living inside.

This agent was as enjoyable a character as my previous one wasn't. When we entered the cabin, it was like walking into a garage, one large room with exposed framing and black paper between the studs. The ceiling had some nice wood on it, but there were no interior walls, no insulation, and no lights, just an empty shell. The owner had left a wooden desk, a metal frame for a box spring and mattress, and a mysterious plastic laundry tub without any connection to water. It had a minimal survivalist spirit.

For an ordinary city person, this would have been appalling. But for me, this was more luxurious than any campsite. Here could be a roof over my head, and there didn't seem to be any creatures living inside. The four windows were shuttered so tightly I had no idea how light coming in might affect the place, but that was a small matter.

The agent seemed to know about construction and showed me how the diagonal cross-pieces stabilized the studs. He touted the cement foundation and said the place was solidly built. Being a neophyte in this matter, I had to take his word for it. I'd done enough shopping around to know the property was what I wanted. I told him I was interested, but would have to sleep on it and get back to him.

He had no idea I literally meant what I said. He locked the door, said goodbye, and drove off. I looked one more time at the exterior. I wasn't thrilled with its gray and white exterior, not very desert-like, but I could change that. When I turned to see the mountains in the distance, the view was breathtaking. I'd sleep there in my car that night, and if all went well, I'd make him an offer the next day.

After eating dinner nearby, I drove back to the cabin. The dirt roads were not easy to negotiate in the dark, but they were full of adventure. I parked my car in front of the house and took a short walk. Morongo Valley has very few residences and hardly any electric light, leaving the nighttime sky full of stars and constellations. It was a bit scary. I had no idea what desert creatures would hang out there. Yet, there was magic in the air. I returned to my car, pulled back the seat and covered myself with a comforter.

No sooner than I had fallen asleep when I was awakened by the glare of headlights and the sound of a vehicle's engine. I hoped it wasn't the police. A man had gotten out of his truck and was rapping on my window wanting to know what I was doing there. I told him I was thinking of buying the cabin and was spending the night to get the feel of the place. I told him I was no threat, maybe a potential neighbor. He wanted to make sure I wasn't some riff-raff trying to do damage. When I assured him I wasn't, he became friendly, wished me a good night, and drove away. Little did I know, this man would become more than a neighbor, but also a good friend and a mentor.

It was a quiet night, the only sounds being that of a few coyotes howling in the distance. The hustle and bustle of city life slowly was replaced by a peacefulness and wholeness that had been missing in my life. Enjoying the simplicity of being connected to the earth below and stars above, I slept very well.

As I woke up early, golden light filled the valley, the sun rising over the eastern hills, gradually transforming the landscape from muted to bright colors. It was autumn, a perfect time to be out in the desert, not hot and not yet cold. One could hear the cars on highway 62 over a half-mile away, but the sounds were muffled enough to be pleasant.

The nearest structure was an abandoned mobile home on piers. Two neglected shacks nearby were also in bad shape. The closest houses in any direction that appeared to be lived in were over two blocks away. Most of the dry wash in front of the cabin was part of the property, so my stunning view was certain to remain undisturbed. Although I was seeking solitude, there was enough of a sparse community here that I wouldn't be too alone. A few miles over the hill was Yucca Valley. A short distance in the other direction was the more sophisticated Coachella Valley. This quasi-seclusion not too far from civilization seemed to be a perfect balance.

Negotiating A Sale

I called the agent and asked if the price was flexible, saying I wanted to make an offer. He replied that there was some room for negotiation. The owner was so anxious to sell he even offered to finance the property, taking payments over time. I was advised to schedule an appointment soon, since a few other people had also shown interest in the cabin. We shook hands over the phone.

Back in LA, I went over my options. I could afford the place, even if I had to use a credit card advance to purchase it. A better choice would be to get a line of credit against the home I already owned. Having been turned down for this in the past when my credit was in bad shape, I had taken great pains in the preceding few years to remedy this. Living an austere life, I'd worked around the clock to pay down my debt. This time, when I went into my bank to request a loan, instead of being turned down as in the past, it was Mr. Cohen this and Mr. Cohen that. My debt to income ratio was in such good condition, that within an hour I had the line of credit in the bag. I would not only able to confidently offer a deposit to hold the property, I had enough funds at my disposal to purchase it for cash.

Due to the unstable financial climate at the time and my ability to pay in full, I was in a good bargaining position. I offered the owner $13,000, fully expecting that he'd meet me in the middle at $15,000. I got a response right away that my offer was accepted just as it was. At first, I was exhilarated. Then I tried to come down to earth quickly, having recently been through escrow disappointment. Yet, things seemed to be on a much better track than before.

How Gray Green Was My Escrow

My second attempt at Morongan escrow was a simpler affair. This jovial agent was a pleasure to do business with, knowledgeable in many practical matters. He gave me helpful pointers on future utility connections. Natural gas was not available, so I would need propane. Water would either have to be delivered monthly to a storage unit or I could invest in drilling a well. Hooking onto the electricity grid could be somewhat costly, as I was two blocks from the nearest electric pole. At that time my plans were merely to camp out in the cabin, so I put off these decisions until later.

The agent connected me with an escrow company in Palm Springs, and things ran smoothly. No complications arose, no infirm owner, no conservators, no probate, no court hassles. I had to sign a lot of papers. Government agencies seem to complicate real estate more every year. I had environmental regulations to deal with, proximity to military space, mineral rights and a host of other things. I was not surprised to find that my parcel was in an earthquake zone, but a bit taken aback to learn that it was also in a flood zone. This meant that in a hundred-year rainstorm, the wash might temporarily flood. A friend of mine with building experience inspected the property and assured me that I was high enough on the bluff not to be in any danger. In a worst-case scenario, my acreage would become a temporary peninsula. I joked I could then sell the place then as lakefront property.

A greater concern was vandalism. Vacation homes in remote areas run that risk. I surmised that the tightly nailed window shutters were due to this prospect. I found some broken pieces of glass on the ground, probably the result of a previous break-in. Another security concern was a complete lack of fencing. However, for the time being, I didn't plan to store anything of value in the cabin.

It was a sixty-day escrow, and the two months passed quickly. During this time I was allowed inside to inspect it only twice. These short visits were all I had to get my bearings and make some plans. When I brought a couple of friends out to the place, there wasn't much for us to see besides the view. So I waited.

I rang in the year 2002 full of expectation. The transaction was due to close in mid-January. After only a small delay, I was instructed to wire in the funds, the final papers were signed, and the monies distributed. I met the agent at the property and he handed me two sets of keys. Immediately, the theme song to the movie "Exodus" started playing in my head. The cabin was mine.

My One-Room Haven

I thanked the agent for shepherding me through this process. He smiled affably and waved goodbye. Though not the first house I'd ever bought, this was my first vacation home, the first outside my native metropolis. I proudly entered the residence. The first thing I did was hammer open some shutters to let in the sunlight. Not only was the view amazing, the extra light gave the cabin a wonderful brightness. Now I could fully see the quirky furniture inside. I resolved to buy a mattress for the bed-frame as soon as possible.

It was a great feeling to own the place, modest as it was. So many of my friends lived in nicer homes and drove newer cars than me. They had appliances and gadgets far beyond my scope. But now I owned two residences and felt wealthy indeed. Suddenly, I was overcome with paranoia. Guilt comes easily to me from my ethnic upbringing. If only I'd finished the Jewish religious school my parents had sent me to. If only I hadn't cooked up all that bacon on Yom Kippur. My list of transgressions would take years to atone for.

Then I thought about the broken glass and the shutters. Would I be safe here? Would someone break in during the night or when I was gone?

When would I see my first snake, tarantula, or scorpion? I had a host of demons ready to plague my serenity. Was this the beginning of buyer's remorse, or just a natural sorting out process?

To help dispel these fears I rearranged the furniture, such as it was, to give myself a sense of ownership.   Nailing the shutters back to their original state, I said goodbye and locked the door.   Meanwhile, I congratulated myself for having the courage to act on my dream of land and cabin ownership. I took a deep breath and drove back to LA on white cumulus clouds of pride.

Setting Up A Getaway

Before my first overnight stay, I made a list of what I needed to supplement the camping gear I already owned. Besides my sleeping bag, Coleman lantern and stove, cooler, flashlights, and candles, I bought a mattress and water jugs. Packing some road food, paper plates, and plastic utensils, I was good to go.

Arriving at twilight on a new moon evening, the dark descended quickly. The nighttime sky was pitch black except for an umbrella of stars. Once inside, I lit my candles, assembled my stove, and brewed my first cup of joe, raising my coffee mug to the spirits of the night in a celebratory salute. Sleeping alone with my door and windows closed, I hardly heard a thing. The silence was deafening. No traffic noise leaked in from the highway, no city static or police helicopters interrupted the quiet.

It was both comforting and disconcerting to be alone where everything was so still. Like a junkie withdrawing from too much stimulation, I slept in fits and starts, awakened in the middle of the night by the sounds of coyotes howling and local dogs barking. By early morning, it was downright cold. I stuffed myself deep into my sleeping bag resolving to bring some extra blankets for my next stay.

At dawn I brewed some coffee, cooked some oatmeal, and sat outside my cabin. The air was brisk as the sun rose over the eastern hills, shining on the western parts of the valley a half-hour before lighting up the area near my new residence. I watched the sunlight creep up from the outskirts of my acreage towards me. It wasn't until the first rays shone on the cabin that the air started to warm.

Taking a short hike, I explored my new neighborhood. A few blocks away I climbed a hillside to get a better view. Several large eucalyptus trees bordering someone's driveway inspired me to plant some myself. Returning to the house, I made notes for what I needed to make the place more functional.

One of my first tasks was to set up a working toilet facility, not an easy thing without available water. I'd been commuting to a Del Taco restroom four miles away in Yucca Valley, but needed something for more immediate needs. I discovered that for $50 a month I could rent a porta-potty from a local company, but for my very limited use, this cost was a bit steep. Since this was frontier living, I had to learn to be resourceful. So I created what turned out to be a successful alternative. I warn any readers who are squeamish to skip over the next paragraph (Mom, if you ever get a copy of this book in the Hereafter, skip this part immediately).

In a thrift shop, I found a commode with a toilet seat infirm people use near their bedsides and purchased it for $10. Then I bought four large wooden poles and hammered them into the ground to make a five by five foot square. Stapling some fabric around the poles, I fashioned a cloth flap for a door. Digging a large hole in the middle of my improvised bathroom, I placed the commode above it. As a cat owner and dog sitter, I knew that animal poop is easily dispensed with in plastic bags and thrown in the trash. I had no thought of doing this with human remains as biological deposits in the desert dry up fast or are scavenged. However, paper does not easily biodegrade. So I bought some aromatic trash bags for paper disposal and let nature do the rest.

This method may not get the Good Housekeeping Seal of Approval, but it worked. I'd read that liquid soap like Dove helps to disintegrate whatever one leaves in an outhouse bottom. I filled the commode pail with TP, bottled water, aromatic bags, and a container of Dove. For several years, I used this waterless closet without any problems.

Most of my friends were happy I had gotten myself a vacation home, but not many were eager to spend overnight in such primitive surroundings. A few said they'd stay with me once I got indoor plumbing, which wasn't going to be anytime soon. So, although I had my share of guests who visited for the day, only a rugged few were willing to stay with me there overnight.

I had an idea that the 12-year-old son of a friend of mine would enjoy this kind of adventure. He and I already had gone on a few camping trips together. When I asked him, he said yes, and his mom gave the OK. On our first stay, we packed sleeping bags and extra blankets for the cold. I also brought along a small futon from LA for him to sleep on comfortably.

It was mid-February and a cold spell had hit the desert with a relentless freezing north wind. Inside the cabin, the thin siding hardly blocked the cold. I'll never forget waking up in the middle of the night to go outside to take a whiz. A thermometer I had placed outside read 28 degrees Fahrenheit. I thought 'yellow snow" was reserved for mountain areas, but the high desert has seen me contribute my share.

In the morning, we lit a campfire to warm ourselves while I made some coffee and cocoa. That night, I bought some marshmallows, graham crackers and chocolate for s'mores. It was a fun weekend. He accompanied me here several more times in the next few years.

As the climate warmed, I bought a patio dining table and chairs, preparing for more company. The springtime air was delightful. A pleasant breeze blew through the valley every afternoon. After researching the web on desert landscaping, I planted several drought resistant trees - palo verdes, mesquites and Aleppo pines. To these I added four eucalyptus like ones I had seen nearby, and a desert olive, a tree a close friend had recommended (more on this later). I filled my jugs in the water machines in town to give these new plants the moisture they required, looking forward to greenery and shade.

One day, the same man who'd stopped me on the sleepover before I bought the place came by for a visit. He liked that I was bringing trees to the neighborhood and invited me to use his well to fill my jugs. He even volunteered to water my trees when I was away for any length of time. This became the start of a valued friendship.

Painting And Insulation Parties

During my first year, I visited the cabin regularly to make improvements. Often I brought along friends who also enjoyed the desert and were brave enough to weather the elements. One of these friends was someone I'd met in my sweat lodge days, a nature lover with a real pioneer spirit. The dirt roads in my neighborhood reminded her of the washboards, as she called them, of her childhood days in South Dakota. One day when she and I were having breakfast, my neighbor stopped by with a friend, also a neighbor. They invited us over for beer and music. This area was getting downright friendly.

Another of my buddies liked to kick back here and forget about his responsibilities in town. We'd go to the mineral springs nearby and out to dinner, or sometimes cook up a camp meal at my cabin. He helped me make a barbecue area out of cement bricks and two metal grills. Now I could grill chicken, ribs or steaks instead of just eating out of cans. Life was good. I was feeling quite at home.

As summer arrived, the heat got intense, though not as oppressive as the lower desert with its daytime highs above 110 degrees. Morongo's 100-degree readings in July and August were hot enough. Although the sun can drain one's energy, the saving grace here was the daily afternoon breeze. The way to take advantage of this was to stay in the shade and let the winds do their cooling. The inside of the cabin got hot as well, especially later in the day and at night.

The hot dry weather was challenging, but even worse was the monsoonal moisture that sometimes blew in from the southeast drenching the place in tropical heat. Instead of dropping down to the usual 70 degrees, the breezeless nighttime monsoon air rarely dipped below 85. On these evenings, the cabin became a virtual steam bath. I wasn't comfortable sleeping outside because of the coyotes, so I had to suffer indoors during these periods. I resolved to look into building an overhang to cool the place down.

A friend suggested I insulate the cabin to mitigate the extreme climate. I didn't need convincing. Like Tom Sawyer and his fence that needed painting, I put the word out to friends I'd exchange a free weekend in the desert with meals, hot springs and lodging for help installing the insulation. Two buddies took me up on this. We had fun alternating between hard work and cold beverage breaks, ending with some barbecue and R&R. When the project was completed, my friendships were stronger and the cabin was cooler. I hoped this would also provide greater protection from the winter cold.

This barter system was so successful I extended the practice to some painting parties. I disliked the cabin's grey and white Cape Cod colors, preferring to make my little shack blend in with its surroundings. I have a friend who is a painter for the movie studios and an expert in mixing colors. I took him a sample of sand from my parcel, and asked him to make a match, which he did. These parties really changed the look of the place. Celebrating afterwards at a neighbor's house, my friends and I toasted the transformation with some brewskis and raucous laughter.

These neighbors would drop by from time to time, invariably bringing a couple of six-packs of beer. Because I'm such a lightweight, they easily outdrank me five-to-one. Although I'd just as soon have had apple juice, in this redneck environment I didn't want to ruffle any feathers. I did turn down their regular cigarettes, as well as an occasional hit from a more powerful, if not legal, roll-up. I'm neither a churchgoer, nor an imbiber. In these western environs, the modus operandi is "live and let live". Despite some differences, we all got along nicely.

That winter, I was more prepared for the cold. With the new insulation, the wind no longer whistled through the cabin. It got frosty, but not the bone chilling temperatures of the previous year. Using a propane heater for a few hours late at night and first thing in the morning also helped to make the cabin more comfortable.

A Housewarming And A Memorial

In March, when the weather was more hospitable, I invited several of my LA friends over for a housewarming. For most, this would be just for the day, since staying overnight was too primitive. We had a potluck lunch, and shared a memorial service for two close friends who had passed away that winter within a week of each other.

Emotions were mixed as we celebrated their lives and acknowledged their departure by planting and dedicating a tree to each. An Aleppo pine became a tribute to our dear woman friend and the desert olive honored our male friend. I had spoken to this man only days before his sudden death. Because he was an avid gardener, I asked him what trees he would recommend here. He suggested the desert olive, hence the dedication. At the memorial, his son placed some of his dad's ashes in the soil around the olive tree. Other friends buried remembrances at the tree bases as well.   It was a very touching ceremony. I still think of these friends whenever I look at these trees.

Building A Patio

My second summer was approaching. Having conquered the cold, I was determined to beat the heat. One day I asked my neighbor for advice on how to create more shade. He'd worked construction, and I admired the craftsmanship of the work he'd done on his own house. He suggested I have a concrete slab poured for a patio, and he would help me build an overhanging roof. Liking the idea, I agreed to hire him as soon as he was available.

It wasn't long before I went to a home improvement store "down below" with his list of materials. In a few days everything was delivered to my place. Then I called a concrete man he'd recommended, and soon the man and his assistant came over to frame the porch one day and poured cement the next. What a change. The slab was almost as large as the cabin itself.

We started working on the overhang two days later, after giving the slab enough time to dry. My friend hammered four large weight-bearing posts into the cement, spaced about eight feet apart, and then joined them with cross pieces. He added connecting rafters and overhead plywood sheets. I was his willing and grateful assistant in awe of his confident, graceful ability to hammer in countless nails, hardly ever missing the mark. The following weekend I brought my South Dakotan friend over for additional help. She and I painted the wood with a primer, followed by a bright white top coat.

The next step in this process was tarpapering the roof. We laid down some roofing sheets. I glued, he nailed. I got an education in how many different kinds of nails one uses in construction. There were galvanized, common, box, roofing and several others, all in various lengths and widths. For someone who'd never done anything like this before, and who always considered himself to be all thumbs when it came to mechanical work, this was an awesome accomplishment. My neighbor was also pleased.

When we finished the overhang, the place looked fantastic. The cabin was now much cooler, and I had additional room and shade where I could enjoy my glorious vista. From the road, it was gratifying to see my humble abode had become doubly wide. Not bad for just over $2,000. Life was good and getting better.

More Company And More Comfort

During this period I added some new names to my guest list. Each of them contributed ideas for improving the place. Some even donated furniture and household items making it more livable.

An old college roommate and lifelong friend who lives in Wisconsin and teaches at the university level came for a visit. An artist and set designer, he gave me some decorating ideas, like stapling fabric on the ceiling and putting light wood paneling over the insulation. He also gave me a drawing he had done of me back in our UCLA days. I immediately hung it on the wall. Later that year I acted on many of his suggestions, giving the cabin an arty feel.

One autumn weekend I had a slumber party at my cabin. The guests were the young man whom I would go camping with, his mom, and a mutual friend of ours. Oh yes, and four dogs. My one large room easily accommodated all of us with our sleeping bags and air mattresses. The pooches especially liked the expansiveness of my acreage to roam around off-leash. The only downside was removing occasional cactus thorns they picked up in their paws.

My sleepover had an unexpected result. It solved a difficult situation for my young camping buddy's mom. Finances necessitated a move. When she saw that rents in the Morongo Basin were far less than in LA, she considered relocating here. Her work transcribing documents on her computer gave her the freedom to establish a home base anywhere. I helped her scout out rental houses nearby and she moved to city of Joshua Tree, twelve miles away.

I never thought she was the desert type. Born in Sweden, she was a cold weather gal, not someone who liked hot summer temperatures. Despite having tastes much more sophisticated than redneck, once she recovered from the culture shock, she became a real fan of the desert. Taking her dogs for a walk along the hiking trails next to Joshua Tree National Park, she'd talk enthusiastically about our natural beauty and dramatic weather. Having her living nearby strengthened the growing bonds I was making in the area.

By now, I had achieved a level of comfort within my primitive confines. One day, the friend who'd built my cement block barbecue showed me how to use a 12-volt car battery and an inverter to run electric lights to replace the candles and lanterns. I wouldn't say I was stylin', but I had established a solid home away from home. For the next few years I maintained my cabin as it was. I had no reason to take it to the next level.   It remained this way until my living situation in Los Angeles provoked me to make some changes.

The house was quiet and the world was calm.
The reader became the book,
And summer night was like the conscious being of the book.
The house was quiet and the world was calm.

Wallace Stevens

Original Cabin On The Bluff

Original cabin exterior

Original cabin interior

Early cabin decor

Cabin interior a little later

Painting the exterior

Cabin with patio and overhang

PART 4 - TEMP TO PERM MAKEOVER

Plan A – Adding 3 Rooms
An Empty Cabin

I was in the process of retreating from my urban life style, but only up to a point. Old habits were hard to change. My temporary getaway was a fine refuge, but anytime I'd think about making a complete break from the city, I'd run into resistance.

From 2003 until 2006, I put the cabin on autopilot. I knew someday I might add to my one room and patio, but I wasn't ready to invest the energy and funds to change the place much. I'd drawn up plans to add a kitchen, dining room and bathroom, another 400 square feet, and even sketched placement of these new rooms and the views out of each window. Yet I had reservations about what this might cost.

My cabin frequently sat unused during this time. The extreme temperatures in winter and summer often made the house uncomfortable. Other California natural beauty spots such as the mountains and beaches called to me instead of the desert. All my relatives had moved out of LA, and I needed to travel far to visit them. This all cut back the time I spent at my desert sanctuary. It sometimes was vacant for a whole month or even longer.

For a while, I considered selling the place. Real estate was going up everywhere in California. The desert was no exception. It was getting so pricy by the coast that many people looked inland for cheaper alternatives. Even without utilities, I could have let my property go for quite a profit. However, I held onto it as a safe haven, or when I would visit friends in the area. As I did, in the back of my mind, I'd wonder what it would be like if my cabin had a real kitchen and bathroom with electricity and running water. I certainly enjoyed the more temperate spring and fall months. How much easier would it be to stay there with heat in the winter and air conditioning in the summer? Maybe, I'd visit year round. Perhaps someday I might even want to live in it full time.

I knew getting connected to the grid for electricity or going solar could mean ten thousand dollars. Having a well dug and getting plumbing would cost much more, not to mention the price of construction, which was rising every year. As I approached sixty, though I'd think about relocating in the desert, I wasn't ready to leave LA. I tabled that until, like the Beatles said so eloquently in song, "When I'm Sixty-Four".

Contemplating Early Exodus

Several things occurred that made me consider speeding up my timetable. The music business went through some big changes. With the popularity of free downloading on the internet, music sales were falling. Recording acts were writing most of their own material, so the market for original songs plummeted. Songwriting classes, where I had been making much of my living, followed a similar decline. Seeing my income taking a plunge, I was led to contemplate retiring (or semi-retiring) earlier.

Another factor making relocation more attractive was that it was getting more expensive to live in LA. Property taxes were increasing, as was the price of insurance, gasoline, food, utilities, trash pickup and seemingly everything else. I was becoming house-rich/cash-poor. Gridlock was getting unbearable. The commute to my students and classes was taking longer and getting more stressful with each passing year. I was paying more for a smaller slice of marble cake. My cabin started looking increasingly like a viable alternative, but turning sixty-four was still a few years away. Meanwhile, my life was getting more and more frustrating.

A New Best Friend

During this time a new addition came into my life that helped mitigate this situation.   My Joshua Tree friend had scraped enough money together to buy a house. Her son, who by now was in his teens, routinely would rescue animals and bring them home for adoption. She added a new dog, two cats, a parrot, and even a rat to their menagerie. One day when I was visiting, he brought over an adorable dark brown female pit bull that was just over a year old. Ignored by its owners, the dog was skinny and somewhat frightened, but very affectionate. The minute she saw me, the animal came right over and licked my face. I had health and financial problems at the time, and appreciated the loving attention she gave me.

Her son begged for yet another pet, but my friend put her foot down. She asked me to take the dog to the animal shelter in Yucca Valley. I was reluctant to do so, because pit bulls are often the first animals to be put down. I relented. On the way to the shelter, the animal kept making eyes at me. In my vulnerable state, I started to fantasize about bringing her home instead.

Although I had two cats at home, this dog was the kind of mid-sized pet I preferred, not a lap dog, but not too large. I had a fenced yard she could stay in, and I could benefit from the lift she might provide. At the shelter, I was about to put her in the overnight cage for drop-offs when I decided to bring her home for a trial. This was one of my best decisions. I met her the day Marlon Brando died, and named her Stella, after the movie clip from "A Streetcar Named Desire" that the news programs ran that week. I've never had a better companion, as she became all a man's best friend could ever be.

Expansion Plans

Not long after I integrated Stella into my life, on a whim I got out some drawings I'd made for the three rooms I'd wanted to add to the cabin. I had long thought about knocking out a wall to create an entrance to a kitchen area on the south side of my building. In front would be a dining room with a picture window to face my incredible view. Behind all this I could build a bathroom. I had that in mind when I planted my trees, positioning them to give shade, yet allow for expansion someday and still see my panoramic vista.

I went over my bank statements to see what I'd be comfortable laying out for this. As a writer, there was always a chance I'd get a lucky break, adding to what I was receiving for placing a few of my songs in films. I'd even recorded an album of my own work that got critical rave reviews, but no rave royalties were rolling in to support it. Without any fat checks arriving in my mailbox, I realized my home equity was my best source of funds. Yet, any real expansion would require paying the equivalent of two mortgages. Without some new financial infusion, I might have to sell one of my properties to retain the other. Facing this fork in the road, I decided to go ahead with the project and accept the consequences.

Inspector's Warning

When I discussed my decision with the neighbor who had built my patio overhang, he was delighted to hear this. He'd been working as a realtor, doing occasional construction jobs on the side. Both businesses were slow. When I asked if he wanted the job, he was happy to get the work. I showed him my plans, and he advised me to talk to the Building And Safety people in Yucca Valley about getting a permit, or they might disallow this. I soon found that owning property doesn't give one license to do whatever one wants with it. You have to get government permission for almost everything.

I made an appointment to have an inspector come out for what they call a preconstruction permit. My neighbor had told me that two inspectors worked in that office, one much easier to deal with than the other. Someone must have been watching out for me, because the man who arrived at the cabin was an easygoing guy, obviously the nicer of the two men. But when he read my plans, he saw right away that I hadn't factored in considerations such as setback requirements. All permanent structures have to be at least 55 feet from any roads or easements, paved or otherwise.

My original structure had been built right at the limit of two of these setbacks. There was no room for any construction to the south or to the east. At once, the designs I had been carrying in my mind for such a long time were negated. To the west, my bluff descended to the wash, so there was not much area to build there either. All I had left was about fifty feet to the north.

In my mind, I quickly repositioned the three rooms into a northern expansion, and mentioned this to the inspector. He warned me that since I was in a flood zone, I'd have to meet FEMA requirements. When I said my cabin was high enough to be out of harm's way, he replied that when it comes to government regulations, this didn't make any difference. Writing down a phone number of an office in San Bernardino, he told me to consult with them before getting my hopes up. He filled out some papers, gave me a copy, and muttered that flood-zone residences need to be elevated. There was a possibility that I might have to build an entirely new building. Any new residence would have to be at least 750 square feet in size. He smiled weakly and left.

I was crestfallen. This was America, a free country and the government was telling me what I could and couldn't do with my own property. He was the nicer of the inspectors. What if the stern guy had met me instead? I called my neighbor to get his input. He told me to get ready for more of this. Even though his home is situated on a hill fifty feet higher than mine, he also had problems with FEMA. His house technically was also in the same flood zone, and he had to get waivers to do improvements there.

FEMA Pulls The Plug

Stopping at the FEMA office on the way home, the engineer there gave me more disappointing news. Because of my flood zone status, I could only add on 15% of the value of my original residence. My cabin was an empty shell and worth little. At that rate, I couldn't even add a tool shed. I pleaded that my building was well above any flood area. He said those were the rules and warned that any new construction had to be raised 2 feet off the ground. The only way I could incorporate my cabin into a new building was to elevate the building. I told him it was built on a slab. He said I'd have to raze it and start over. Or, if I had room, I could construct an entirely new building near it, as long as it was not attached to the original one.

I left San Bernardino in state of shock. A new 750 square foot structure would eat up most of my home equity, severely limiting my options. My dream of retiring early was fading fast. This was only the first in a series of disappointments I was going to have to endure.

A Neighborly Suggestion

On the way home, tears rolled down my cheeks. If lemons were being thrown in my path, I had to make some lemonade. When I shared my disappointment with my neighbor, he suggested that if a new residence was too expensive, maybe I could keep the cabin as it was and set a manufactured home next to it. Pre-fab houses were less per square foot to construct than stick-built residences. Perhaps I could have two buildings.

This rekindled my hopes. I'd already done some research on manufactured homes. On the way back into town I stopped at a pre-fab home dealer to get a handle on the current scene. The salesgirl in the office showed me some new and used mobile homes available. When I heard the phrase mobile home, I grimaced. How poignant to spend my golden years as trailer trash. Yet I was determined to see if this could work. When I climbed onto the manufactured home bandwagon, little did I know what a roller coaster ride I was getting myself into.

For every room a house has a parlor, bed-room,
And dining-room thrown pell-mell in the kitchen.
And now and then a smudged, infernal face
Looked in a door behind her and addressed her back.
She always answered without turning.

Robert Frost

Plan B – Trailer Trash Nightmare
Manufactured Homes On The Net

The thought that I might spend the rest of my life in an overgrown trailer with vinyl wallpaper and tacky fixtures filled me with trepidation. I tried to find comfort in the words of the Rolling Stones, "You don't always get what you want, but if you try sometimes, you get what you need." I had to go on faith that something better might turn up. Taking myself out for a nice dinner at a fancy Mexican restaurant, I drowned my sorrows in a margarita, chips, salsa, and combination plate. Calorie-wise, this was an indulgence, but if I was going to be "white trash", I might as well eat, drink, and look the part.

After dinner, I got out paper and a pen and began designing my ideal manufactured home. I positioned the living room, dining area, and kitchen so they faced my great view. For the bedroom, bathroom, and an office, this didn't matter. Since I already had the cabin, the house only needed to be the minimum 750 square feet. I had limited space that would not accommodate more than this footage anyway. Little by little, I worked out a floor plan. Being the creative type, I don't care whether my media is words and music, or walls, doors and windows. As the margarita danced in my brain, I soon had something quite impressive, at least to me. I'd be stylin' in my trailer, so there. Hell, I was not going to spend any more than I had to just to fit some damn government edict (I am such a lightweight drinker that alcohol had released the profane side of my nature).

Returning to LA, I researched the internet for manufactured homes. Almost all featured houses were well over 1000 square feet, most over 2000. This mansionization of trailerhood was in full swing. The only small ones that I saw were what are known as single wides, one room in width. Morongo Valley doesn't permit these skinny homes, so I had to find a small double wide, if there was such a thing. Visiting one website after another, the few modest-sized floor plans available had several tiny rooms meant for munchkins.

Then I saw one that shocked the heck out of me (the alcohol had worn off, and so had my profanity). It was an 800 square foot double-wide, not with the 2 bedrooms that I'd designed, but one large bedroom and an open living-dining-kitchen area that faced out to the rear where I could take advantage of the view. It was amazingly similar to what I had drawn. I didn't need two bedrooms, since I had the cabin. The least expensive home in their catalog, its dimensions fit perfectly on my available space. It seemed to be heaven sent.

This southern Utah company's website had detailed photos with many features and options. One could buy a manufactured dream house. My call was referred to a personable salesman who had just built a house in the desert himself. He was full of information. Like a butcher who hawks how fresh his meat is, he sang the praises of the exciting materials contained in their homes. He said I needed to get in on the ground floor soon. These houses were in high demand, and their prices were going up fast. In retrospect, I'm surprised he didn't try to sell me a time-share on the Brooklyn Bridge. My enthusiasm for this one floor plan was so intense, I must have been like my dog when she sees a stick being thrown for fetching. Since the company wasn't local, I asked to see one of their homes in California. He said there was an open house not far from me just north of the desert hamlet of Mojave. I asked for and was emailed directions.

Open House On The Desert

I could hardly wait to visit the open house. I brought along the friend who had helped me build the brick barbecue and install the 12-volt lighting system. He always had good practical sense.

Mojave is 100 miles north of LA, California City twenty miles further. The house was better than I expected. From the street, with its dormers and exterior stucco, you'd hardly know the building was manufactured. I suspected it would be a showcase for the high end of the company's line in order to sell homes, and I was right. The walls were tape and textured, the kitchen had impressive appliances, and the bathroom had a nice tiled tub enclosure. The light fixtures were better than the tacky ones I'd feared.

When I asked the agent how much the extras in this model cost, he said only several thousand dollars. He downplayed this. Stucco alone is a few thousand. Yet seeing a real home, not a design on my computer, reinforced the possibility that this could work for me. We discussed my concern about critters getting under the house. He assured me that a bricked-in foundation wall with a locked door hatch under the home would address this, but he was wrong here as well.

On the agent's desk there was a large container of Oreo cookies, which my friend raided. I think the sugar rush dampened my buddy's judgment. He hardly had anything negative to say about the model house. I didn't need any baked goods to dampen my critical mind. Sensing the stars I had in my eyes, the salesman threw me an incentive I couldn't resist. Since I had traveled from LA to see this open house, he'd give me a $2,500 discount if I put down a $5,000 deposit within a week's time. The company had already had offered 15% off for finding them online. It seemed to be quite a bargain.

My father's voice was racing through my head. This was such a deal! Visions of two buildings on my parcel floated through my head. Adding up the square footage, four hundred for the cabin, three hundred for the porch and eight hundred for the manufactured (let's not say mobile) home, I'd have quite a spread where I could entertain many visitors. Maybe the gods were looking out for me.

Negotiating A Sale #2

When I got back to LA, I called the company's Utah office and asked about making a purchase. They'd mail out some forms to look over. If I sent them back with a $5,000 check, they'd price protect the home for 60 days. Costs were rising, over 20% in the past year. This deposit would be good for 12 months. The $2500 discount would only be in effect until the end of the week. I was sure this was the home I wanted, and said to send the documents right away.

I've always been too careful with my funds to fall for anything crass, but I was so excited about this home with the open floor plan, I was easy prey. I completely forgot my parents' purchase of the cheaply built residence we'd lived in when I was in my teens. The gods upstairs must have been laughing themselves silly.

I went over the contract. The house was $46K, having it delivered and set up another ten, and a few extra fees and taxes brought it to $62K. With my discount, this was just over $59K. Not bad for 800 square feet and a slew of fixtures. This was what I had planned to spend to expand my existing structure. Now I would have over 1500 square feet of living area, much larger than my modest bungalow in LA. "If I Were A Rich Man" started playing in my bargain-filled brain. If I could have danced the hora at that moment, I would have. The more appropriate dance at the time would have been "The Hustle."

When I read over the papers, they looked fine. After signing and sending in a deposit, I would have a year before needing to apply it to a purchase. I was so anxious to meet the deadline, I "Signed, Sealed and Delivered" the money right away.

So Many Options, So Little Time

Two days after wiring the funds, I received a receipt along with a booklet explaining step-by-step procedures for purchasing a house, choosing the fixtures and décor, adding options, preparing the site, having it delivered, set up, inspected and ready for occupancy. This seemed to be a very together company.

A few days later I got a call from a pleasant bubbly young lady, my customer service rep. Her job was to help me select appliances, wall textures, flooring, paint colors, and especially upgrades. She emailed me a 30-page document with photos of decorated rooms, color and texture samples, countertops, cabinets, carpet and linoleum, and of course, more upgrades. There was so much to choose from, I felt like it was Christmas in May.

I started circling items on every page in a selection frenzy. In addition to what came standard, I chose two sliding glass doors, extra windows for cross-ventilation, thicker insulation in the walls, tape and texture to replace the tacky vinyl wallpaper, longer outside eaves, and wiring for a dishwasher, ceiling fan, and extra lighting. Not out to impress, I didn't add to the exterior for curb appeal. Many manufactured home buyers pay as much for extras as for the house itself. My option list was only a few thousand dollars.

Initially, my rep was very patient, helping me sort through these choices. But once she became aware she wasn't going to make a fortune on options commissions, she stopped returning my email questions quickly, and became less available for phone consultation. I asked for referrals for contractors and site preparers in my area, and though she promised to send me a list, I didn't hear from her.

Before I put more money down on the home, I knew I had to get the permit process started with the building and safety people. With only 45 days left of price protection, I needed to get cracking.

Getting A Permit To Get A Permit

The same inspector who had visited me earlier returned to write out a preconstruction manufactured home permit to take into his office. The cost was $50, chump change for what was to follow. A lady behind the desk there handed me reading material for the next hoops to jump through. I'd need a Fire Permit, a Flood Hazard Review, an Elevation Certificate, a Water Permit, and a Drainage Permit. Each of these had to be followed to the letter or they'd be denied; each had their costs. Since this could take some time, I put on my track shoes.

First, I needed a letter of approval from the fire marshal in Morongo Valley. The local office informed me this would cost $500 and take a couple of weeks before he could assess my property. Driving out in mid-week to expedite things, I filled out some forms and left a check in his mail slot. There was delay since his wife was about to deliver their baby. It took three weeks for him to certify the letter. State specifications required me to have a sprinkler system put in the home and I'd need to pay for an inspection after the house was installed to make sure it was done correctly. Also, I'd need a large water storage tank in case of a fire. This all meant more money.

When I called my customer rep, she said sprinkler systems cost an additional $8,000, more than all my other extras put together; good news for her, but bad news for me. When I researched grading and foundation perimeter costs, my inquiry showed an additional $10,000 for this. I asked her again for assistance. For that amount of money, I'd feel more secure with a referral. She promised to get back to me with a list of people I could interview, but once again didn't respond. My $59K house was now $81K and rising. Additional permit costs and school board taxes would soon be staring me in the face. At $86K, what else could I do but bite the bullet and move forward.

Next was the flood hazard report. This required a licensed engineer to certify that my property was safe to build on and wouldn't impede adjacent ones. I asked my neighbor to recommend an engineer. He referred me to a colleague for whom I left three messages that were never returned.

A second referral led to an engineer in Joshua Tree. He took his sweet time before returning my call, then suggested we meet at my property the next day. I drove out mid-week just to see him, but he stood me up, never calling to cancel. When I phoned him later, he promised to drive past my parcel and give me an estimate. When I called after not hearing from him in two days, he said he drove near the place, looked at it from the highway, and there didn't seem to be any problem. The forms I needed might be $2,000. My house is several blocks from the main road. What could he have seen from that distance? I wrote him off.

A third recommendation yielded an engineer who worked for a large company in Palm Springs. He mentioned a $3,000 figure, and said his firm could do it within 10 days. It was getting closer to the end of my price protection, and afraid my housing costs would go up, I figured I'd go with the additional expense on the reports to save money on the house. He said I could trim the price if I mailed him a geologic survey topo map of the area. I sent one off the next day.

Arizona Factory Tour

Meanwhile, I phoned my customer rep and asked her to set up a factory tour appointment at the Arizona plant where my house would be built. She responded promptly with a date and time. It was mid-June, and I wasn't looking forward to traveling 375 miles in the summer heat (Phoenix can get over 110 degrees then). Yet I felt strongly about seeing a home in person before putting down any more funds. I made arrangements for a four-day weekend, including a stay up in the mountains near Prescott, where it would be cooler and more comfortable. I was fortunate to have timed my trip when a cold front blew through the area, bringing the temperatures down into the 90s. I took Stella along since she enjoys car rides, hanging her head out the window to sniff the world as we drive past it. The nicer weather made this easier for both of us.

I left early to get to Phoenix before the hottest part of the day. Arriving at noon, I walked into the manufacturer's large industrial building for my appointment with a long list of questions, bringing my digital camera to take pictures. When I got to the front desk, the secretary said there was no record of me having an appointment. I mentioned the company that had sent me. She had never heard of them. I said I was planning to buy one of their homes and had driven 400 miles for a tour. I begged her to find someone to show me around. She replied most of the people were gone for the day. Maybe she could get someone to give me a tour.

The plant manager had some free time and graciously offered to show me around. He explained step-by-step how their homes were built, starting with the foundation. At each stage, he discussed the processes involved, rightfully proud of his business. I took many photos. Then he showed me some homes with the cabinets and fixtures being installed getting ready to be shipped out. I saw some large trucks with cranes in the parking lot preparing homes to be delivered. He said they build several homes every day. When I told him that the company in Utah wasn't helping me get construction people like I had hoped, he said they were essentially no more than car dealers. He advised not to expect much from them, but instead look in the phone book in my local area for assistance. Then he excused himself and went to a meeting.

The home manufacturing company had an efficient operation, and I was able to examine many of the features and options I'd only seen in brochures. I fell in love with one of the colors they used in some of the homes, a rich shade of desert peach. At the same time, I had qualms about the Utah salespeople, thinking I'd fallen for a slick sales pitch. They hadn't followed through on assistance, and didn't even bother to schedule an appointment here. The manager didn't hold them in high regard.

On many TV and radio talk shows where people call in with problems, it is standard practice to have a buzzer go off when the host warns someone about potential dangers. Such an alarm was sounding for me. I tried not to overreact. It was Friday and I was on vacation. If I wanted to beat the traffic out of Phoenix, I had to hop on the freeway right away. I'd deal with this later.

I drove to Prescott and had a few glorious days. Not only was the weather comfortable, this city had many enjoyable restaurants and parks. It was a dog-friendly place with pit bulls like Stella a popular choice. She got so much attention she was ready for us to move there. It was Arts and Craft Fair Weekend. I bought some items for my new place including an ethnic tapestry to hang on one of its peach colored walls.

Engineering Deep Pockets In Vain

When I returned to LA, I changed my strategy. The dealer was not going to be much help, so I had to find local people with the rest. While I was gone, the survey firm sent me paperwork to mail back with a check. On my answering machine was bad news from the engineer. After reading the topo maps, he said it would cost $2,000 more than he had quoted and take longer. My price protection deadline was getting near, so I called the dealer to request an extension. My salesman was on vacation (probably spending my $5,000 deposit). I was granted 30 more days, but only this once.

Contacting the engineer, I begged that I was a homebuyer, not a large corporation doing an environmental impact study. He said the government required a lot of work on these forms. He'd try to keep the price down but needed a $3,000 retainer, saying they'd bill me for the difference at the end. Anxious to get this process started, I only had 30 days left, so I paid the piper. The next check to the dealer for 50% of the home's cost would be over $30K.

The engineering firm sent out a team of people and all was in full swing. However, one of the surveyors had a death in the family. Then, two long holiday weekends put people out of commission. The engineer went on vacation (spending his share of my retainer, I presume). It was taking longer and costing me a fortune. When he got back from his break, his rested voice contrasted with my disturbed demeanor. He reassured me they'd be through soon and the project would come in under $5,000. This seemed a little better.

I phoned Building and Safety to say I'd be coming in soon with the certificates. The woman looked up my permit on her computer and said I didn't need these reports. I screamed angrily. Did she mean I spent all that money needlessly? When asked who requested the surveys, I replied that she did, which she denied.

I was so furious I went over her head, calling the San Bernardino office. I was connected to a woman in Victorville who oversaw building and safety in the county. She said the reports were a matter of discretion by the local office, but might be a good idea. I cried on her shoulder, telling her my story in a nutshell. She said if I stayed within the square footage of the original cabin, I wouldn't need the reports because pre-existing structures are grandfathered. I was flabbergasted. After thanking her profusely for her assistance, when I hung up the phone, Stella once again had to lick tears off my face.

The Stubborn Garage Door

As if this drama wasn't enough, I'd been spending time getting my LA home in shape for a potential sale. I painted the exterior in colors I thought would be attractive to a new buyer and spruced up some garden areas. Painting and landscaping were both activities I could do myself, and my limited work situation allowed me to do this. The house was starting to look sharp. For more home improvement, I decided to buy a new garage door. My old one had functioned for many years, but when it broke I opened it manually. Now I could add value and reinstall a convenience I'd long missed.

A garage door company ran ads selling these at $500, which I knew was a teaser rate. My garage wasn't standard, and I'd probably need a custom door. When the salesman told me it would cost more, I wasn't surprised. With a new opener and safe release attachment, the price nearly tripled. The man assured me I'd be getting my money's worth. Since I was buying this as an investment, I paid retail. I could feel my poor father turning over in his grave.

I put down a deposit. The following week, an installer removed the old door and put in a new one. It was a big improvement, except that the door was crooked. He said this was because my garage was not straight due to some hilltop settling. There was nothing he could do then, but if I called the company, they'd send someone to fix it later.

When I reached a representative, I threatened to withhold payment until it was fixed, but they said only after I paid in full would they would send out a repairman. Then, they would make sure it was done correctly. Exasperated, I wrote out a check for the balance. The company did try to fix this. One expert after another came out to make adjustments. After several futile attempts, it functioned OK, but still was crooked.

The complications from what I thought would be a simple purchase made me paranoid about the new house I was buying. I'd read a few nightmare scenarios on the internet about people who had problems with their manufactured homes. It is a common practice in the industry to start the warranties the day the house is paid for, long before it is made ready for occupancy. This process can take months. Many people didn't find dysfunctions in their residences until their warranties had expired. I didn't want to be in that situation.

Cutting My Losses

If a simple garage door had so many problems, a pre-fab home could be much worse. I'd have to hire many strangers before it would be ready to live in with no idea what complications would arise. The salespeople seemed flaky. I was so upset, by the time the engineer called to request his balance, I was livid. Not at him, but at the situation. He wanted $2200 more for the flood certificate.

I weighed buying the manufactured home and limiting myself to a cabin rehab. Ever since I was told I could rebuild my original residence without so much craziness, I kept thinking I'd be better off scaling back my expectations. 400 feet is large for a getaway, but tiny for a house even with 300 square feet of patio space to screen in. Perhaps I could add a couple of rooms there instead. Making a few sacrifices now might avoid potentially big problems ahead.

I called the inspector for advice. He said that on a rehab, I could do what I pleased with the cabin, subject to a few codes. There were guidelines for plumbing, electricity, heating, and insulation, but they were less difficult than for new construction. If I kept the utilities inside the cabin, I'd have more latitude. I could build over the patio slab, but have to extend it two feet for a foundation for new walls. Two feet westward would add 50 square feet to my small residence, not a bad idea.

Staying within my original building, I'd sacrifice a lot of living space and have to write off the $5,000 deposit. Having been a cheapskate all my life, this was excruciating to contemplate. To put this in Catholic terminology, for someone Jewish it was more than a venial sin, more than cardinal. This was mortal. As a child, I was upbraided for paying retail when I could have gotten a discount. Here, my mistakes would cost me a small fortune.

As painful as this loss would be, I considered the benefits. My construction costs would be reduced. I would not be subject to school taxation. This alone would save $3,000. I'd worked with my neighbor, and knew he was reliable. Less would tend to go wrong. Not subject to as much regulation, I'd be a master of my own destiny.

Another advantage to staying within the confines of my cabin was that I liked being on its cement slab. My neighbors in the area on raised foundations had ongoing problems with rodents that bred under their residences and damaged their cars by chewing on parts, not to mention snakes, spiders and scorpions. A foolproof raised foundation perimeter was impossible. True, I'd be giving up a guest room or office and a space to use solely as a music studio. These had been important priorities, but their price could be huge.

I spent more sleepless nights until I realized that less meant more, quality was more important than quantity. It was time to stop bringing the gods upstairs so much laughter. I kept hearing the lyrics in the song "The Gambler" by Kenny Rogers. "You gotta know when to hold' em and when to fold 'em". I folded.

Plan C – Rehab On The Slab
Permission Quickly Granted

When I used to attend sweat lodges, we prayed to the ancestors for assistance. Now I needed to face my predecessors with the courage of my new convictions. I had to live by my own rules, and this meant saying farewell to being a bargain hunter and gatherer. It was time to get my new house in order.

I was ready to start building and once again asked my neighbor to be my general contractor. He agreed and thought my decision wise, saying it would cost me less in the long run and I'd be happier with the result. Once I got my paperwork together, he'd sit down with me to set up a game plan and refer me to workers for plumbing, electrical, septic and digging a well. I crossed my fingers and prayed to the powers that be to give permission to do this.

I called the engineer to tell the surveyors to stop my flood hazard report. This saved me a few hundred dollars right away. Then I gathered my courage and strode into the Building and Safety office to apply for a cabin rehab permit similar to what I'd originally asked for. The woman behind the desk was in a better mood. I didn't provoke her by complaining about the past. She looked up what was required to redo my cabin and add two new rooms. Within a few minutes, she totaled up the costs, $400. Incredulous, I asked if she left anything out. She replied I'd need a series of inspections along the way, but for expenses and paperwork, that was it.

I had a check drawn to the county at my local bank. Within an hour, the permission I'd been seeking for months was granted. That day I went into a local office supply store to get graph paper for some preliminary drawings. At this friendly business I entered on a day when everything was 10% off, how auspicious. All signs said go.

Making Every Square Foot Count

To celebrate my scaled down plans I took myself out to a salad bar. No more combination Mexican dinners. My new house was going to be smaller, so I'd better not get too large.   Between courses of soup, greens, and low-fat dressing, I started drawing plans. Every square foot had to count. The first thing was to partition the cabin into living, kitchen, and bathroom areas. Originally planned to be additional rooms, the latter two had to be fitted inside. I had just enough space.

The bathroom and kitchen in my LA home also weren't large, but I wanted to make better use of these spaces with more counter space and storage in the kitchen. From the manufactured house I'd learned about appliance placement and shelves. In the bathroom I had my heart set on the tiled tub enclosure I'd seen in the model home.

Placing the bathroom near a planned septic tank and the kitchen next to the bathroom would keep all the plumbing in one area, a money saving technique. Incorporating the openness of my ill-fated double-wide, I drew a pass-through to a future dining area. In the living room facing the front road I put a narrow window to retain privacy, and a large picture window to the south to take advantage of the sunlight. A wood stove would go in the back, a sofa bed in front.

Drawing everything to scale, I white inked changes constantly. When I showed my plans to my contractor, he pointed out where some of my ideas were impractical. This was the start of a dialog between my concepts and reality, not unlike other creative projects I'd done. My musicals had required constant revision. Recording an album was a similar experience. Feedback helped to strengthen my work. I'd wake up in the middle of the night to redraw a wall, window or door. When in creative mode, we artists are incorrigible.

This was one of my most rewarding experiences. Showing these designs to knowledgeable people for input was a joy. I sifted through suggestions and made improvements when warranted. As in other creative efforts, much of what I started with saw its way into the final product, while much was changed. The project developed a life of its own. Little of this would have happened if I'd purchased the manufactured home. I sketched plans for two rooms over the previous patio area for dining and sleeping. Outside, I arranged some future outdoor patios.

Home Depot University And Lowe's State College

Having survived Manufactured Home Community College, I was ready to matriculate at Residential Construction University. My contractor gave me my first work assignment to study building supply diversity. He asked me to purchase 2 by 4s, 2 by 2s, studs, z-bars, nails, adhesives, contact paper, shims, and more. I had to pour over the course textbook to make countless decisions for what I wanted inside the cabin. The selections with my pre-fab home couldn't begin to compare the spectrum of choices I had in front of me.

Entering the giant home improvement store campuses, I felt like a freshman. I consulted with a variety of employees, grateful to many for being such patient teachers. It was as if I had to enroll in a class for each part of an enormous jigsaw puzzle I was putting together. Kitchen 101 included appliances, cabinets, sinks, faucets, and countertops. Bathroom 1A focused on bathtubs, wall enclosures, toilets, vanities, mirrors, and medicine chests. Living Room 400 was an independent study course. Electives included wood stoves and swamp coolers. The Interior Lecture Series covered doors and windows, while Exterior Workshops went over siding, budget and priorities. With this heavy course load, I was a full-time student.

I learned the difference between base cabinets, sink base cabinets, blind corner base, drawer, wall, and bridge wall cabinets. Combining these in various sizes I matched my kitchen area, wall and ceiling space, and appliances. I needed to choose wood finishes, and then cap them off with the right color and design of countertops in the appropriate granite, formica, laminate, or marble. Prior trips to these kinds of stores were often undertaken just to choose paint colors. Now I had many so more decisions to make.

At the Sink Lab course I sifted through a variety of acrylic, stainless steel and ceramic sinks. Homework included familiarizing myself with chrome, brass, and satin nickel low and high curved faucets with plastic and shiny metal single and double knobs. Prices varied from bargain basement to middle-of-the-road to semi-deluxe to over-the-top. Some were sale priced, some closeouts, and others special order material.

For the Appliance Workout I made lists of refrigerators, stoves, microwaves, dishwashers, washers and dryers. Each had their features, some basic and some deluxe, some with new gadgets, and many with improvements I was not interested in.   Adding to all these decisions were the special discount offers, deferred payment incentives to buy more, gift cards in return for certain items if bought during a certain week, etc. My bakery bargaining brain went full-tilt.

At the Interior Lecture Seminars we debated windows. There were double-pane, low emission, grid or non-grid, aluminum or vinyl framed, clear or obscure choices.   Most were readily available only in popular sizes. Some windows had to be special ordered. I was surprised to find these custom windows were hardly more expensive than their generic cousins. They just took longer to arrive.

Starting off as a kid in a candy store, I'd arrive home exhausted after spending hours writing down model numbers, features and prices. Which items were best for function, which were only for show, which held up the best, when was it worth it to spend more, and when was this unnecessary? I researched the web, read consumer magazines, and did extracurricular study on the home decorating cable TV channel.

These were all required lower division foundation courses. I hadn't even gotten to the flooring, lighting fixture, and wall decor classes. Fortunately, I was such a diligent student I became fairly knowledgeable in many of these areas. I made the best choices I could, balancing my taste, budget, and practical sense, spending hours with the customer service people in many of these stores. When it was time to cram for final exams, I passed with flying colors.

This several month ordeal was a roller coaster experience. When the coursework was finished, I was ready for a cap, gown and diploma, or at least a hard hat, chainsaw and tool belt. After completing my degree in Home Improvement, my next task was to get a crew and start construction.

<u>Under Construction - 3 Rooms</u>

Bathroom before construction

Kitchen before construction

Front window installation

Electricity installation

Insulation installation

Drywall installation

Kitchen cabinet installation

Well installation

PART 5 - UNDER CONSTRUCTION
Rebuilding The Cabin
My Very Own Porta-Potty

It was time to press full steam ahead. Taking on such a huge endeavor, I had excellent help to guide me. With paperwork in order and design plans drawn, my contractor and I assembled a list of people needed for the project. This included a plumber, electrician, septic tank installer, and someone to drill a well. Before I could hire anyone to build on my property, I was required by the state of California to have toilet facilities available for workers. My "four poles and a hole" wouldn't pass government approval. So I found a portable toilet company, and rented my very own porta-potty.

After years of putting up with primitive bathroom conditions, it was exciting when a truck arrived with a tan fiberglass commode. The driver placed it at one side of the construction area. Setting the structure upright, he outfitted it with TP rolls, and poured chemicals into the basin below. After he departed, I inspected my new latrine. Squeaky clean inside, this new addition had both masculine and feminine symbols printed on the door. How contemporary! Beaming with pride, I went over to my old "outhouse" and disassembled it. I couldn't wait for the first time I would need to use my new toilet. This came soon enough, and I was relieved on more than one level.

Plumbing A Foundation

Now that I had a water closet, the first thing was to find a plumber to set a foundation for the kitchen and bathroom areas. My porta-potty upgrade was only a warm-up for a functional indoor toilet. I'd no longer have to endure extremes in climate when I needed to go. Better yet, I'd be able to entertain potential visitors who'd shunned me because of primitive sanitation facilities. A plumbing technician not only brought keys to more comfort, but also increased popularity.

Fortunately, a skilled plumber lived only two blocks away. This tall, stocky Afro-American man in his forties looked like he could have been a football player in his younger years. I was to learn he indeed had been an athlete who now applied his physical prowess to laying pipes. We made friends instantly, having a common interest in mathematics, mine in making patterns of notes, scales and chords, his in measure pipe connections, water lines, and cleanouts. Since moving to Morongo Valley, he'd established himself as a pipe architect. Like many of the no-nonsense people I was to meet in this area, he knew what to do and did it well.

The contractor, the plumber and I went into a huddle. I was the quarterback who called the shots. Like a good halfback and tight end, they went into formation. Drawing Xs and Os on my slab, we outlined where we'd need to jackhammer through the concrete to set pipes for a sink, dishwasher, washer, dryer, bathtub, toilet and vanity. Other lines would go to an outside water heater and through the cabin studs to a swamp cooler. We created a clean out for servicing near the future septic tank. An additional connection for incoming water from a proposed well was also mapped out. We measured these distances precisely, allowing ground and wall space, a schematic like veins and arteries in one's body.

By putting these areas close together, less and shorter pipe connections were needed than if I had spaced them out. Like someone who buys ground beef in a market and sees no relationship to a cow, I had no inkling how water systems worked. Now I was learning literally from the ground up. The plumber hammered and dug holes in the slab for the pipes. Next, I called an inspector for approval before re-cementing these areas. The same friendly man I'd dealt with before soon arrived. He became a regular visitor for the next few months. We passed the first of many such inspections.

An advantage of downsizing my plans was that I could afford quality materials instead of budget items. The plumber bought some supplies, but I purchased most of the pipes, couplings and fittings for him. I made myself available whenever possible as a deliveryman. This saved time and money. As a by-product, I learned what went into each job. I purchased expensive copper pipes for house lines, specialized green pipe for the gas line, and economical PVC pipe for the outside water line from a well. Within the week we installed the foundation for the house. The rest of the connections would be done after my fixtures and appliances were in.

Framing

The next task was my contractor's specialty, framing. Similarly to how my mom had taught me to select produce in a market, he showed me how to choose the best pieces of wood in a pile of lumber. This was no easy task. Big box stores have many mediocre, even damaged goods in their stacks. In addition to purchasing a long list of products for him, I obtained caps for his nail gun to shoot directly into the concrete. He brought over a collection of electric saws and a generator.

I started making the transition from home improvement dilettante to being one of the professionals. At the contractors' cash register, I scheduled two deliveries for the following week. One big box outfit did a seamless job. The other gave me a nightmare experience.

When the materials arrived, my property was alive with a construction symphony of generator roars, buzzing saws and cap gun shot punctuations. I should have recorded what went on, sampling it on my synthesizer for *musique concrete*. I was almost inspired to grab a baton and start conducting, but my crew would not have understood. Never having been Mr. Macho, I had to cloak the artist in me, as I spent the next several months in machismo territory.

First in were bottom pieces of wood sunk into the cement foundation. Next, studs were nailed into them every sixteen inches, carefully measured to work around the plumbing fixtures. Some walls of the bathroom required six inches of framing for insulation, while others only needed four inches. After every piece of lumber was inserted in place, my builder carefully hammered each board into top and bottom locations. After the studs were solidly fastened, he strengthened them with cross pieces.

Framing the bathroom door was next. I got the idea to add a closet to separate the three rooms, which was well worth the effort. I measured to see how my designs were being realized. The walls were thicker than I'd expected, making the areas a little smaller. Drywall would use even more space. I can see why architects and designers need to factor in many such adjustments.

We needed to take out the old windows to make room for new ones. He removed them one wall at a time, replacing the old frames with new lumber. This took time. The window and door installations went up much faster. The most dramatic change was framing a front door where one had never existed before. I bought a steel door with a leaded glass fanlight on top. When this was in place, it made a big difference. Each new window helped to turn my former primitive cabin into a home.

Sometimes we had to wait for a special ordered window to arrive. These delays gave me time to make changes in their placement. My choice of using long rectangular shapes for their function created a retro style. People would later say the house had a hip design. The last window we added was a rectangle of square acrylic glass blocks, which magnified light coming in. Once finished, we had another inspection, passed easily and were ready for the electrician.

Getting Wired

With the framing set, wiring had to be done before insulation or drywall could be installed. I was unable to reach an electrician suggested by my neighbor. Mentioning this to my plumber, he told me he knew a licensed electrician with many years of experience. When I called this man, we set up an appointment the very morning.

My apprehension hiring a stranger to work in a field I knew little about was eased right away. Very professional and outgoing, he asked detailed questions about what I wanted in the house. This tall lanky man, also

Afro-American, had lived in the area for a few years, but earlier had thriving businesses in Palm Springs and New York City. He suggested items I wouldn't have thought of like track lighting. When I mentioned that I like to cook, he suggested bright fluorescents for the kitchen. He revealed he'd worked as a caterer for some high-end outfits, including serving meals at NFL functions. I'd hired myself a gourmet electrician.

His first task was installing a large meter box outside the cabin for circuits running to various systems inside. On top of this box was a mast that would eventually be connected to the wires coming from power lines Edison had yet to construct. From this meter he wove necklaces of wiring to all parts of the house. Watching him as he worked, I enjoyed the ease with which he threaded and snipped wires. He put in outlets for my appliances, a ceiling fan, a dimmer switch for the track lighting, on/off switches and outlets for each room and plug-ins for outside lights, a swamp cooler, and an electric water heater. Another inspection passed easily. Next was insulation.

Getting Insulated

It had been years since I had insulated the cabin. Over this covering I'd nailed plywood paneling to the studs, knowing it was temporary. Both insulation and paneling had to be removed. The inside of my cabin was strewn with piles of yellow rolls of insulation making it cumbersome to find things inside, scattering residue that was irritating to the skin and, when inhaled, to the lungs. The paneling was tossed outside on a growing scrap heap.

My contractor recommended padding these areas with additional material, as well as stuffing more under the roof between the ceiling rafters for stronger protection from the elements. The inspector might require this anyway. I had additional rolls delivered. We hired a second worker to assist him staple-gun this in place. We got the inspector's approval before continuing. Another slam dunk.

Drilling A Well

This part of Morongo Valley had no municipal water service, so I needed to have a well drilled. My contractor referred me to a man in the area known for his quality work. The guy was so busy I had to reserve his skills weeks in advance. At an interview he said if he drilled 200 feet down, I'd find all the water I could possibly use. My property was on top of a large subterranean lake. The price for materials, labor and permits would be $12,000, about what I had expected. I put down a deposit. Six weeks later he was ready.

This expert and his assistant drove a large truck equipped with a tall crane, which looked like a small version of an oil well rig. After measuring the required 100 feet from my planned septic tank, they set up the equipment and started drilling. It took two days of excavation. Occasionally, things slowed down when they hit a large boulder underneath, unleashing some loud gnashing noises, but soon things would run more smoothly. After the necessary depth was reached to bring the water to the surface, a pump was put in complete with pressure gauges. They capped this with a smooth cement lid.

At the end of the week, they invited me over to watch them pump out the first gush of water. Since I was not yet connected to electricity, a generator was needed to run the pump. A full stream of moisture flowed down to the wash. Cohen Creek was born.

I needed to obtain an environmental agency permit and a bacterial inspection before I could use the well. I was assured once I cleared these hurdles, I'd have enough water to last a lifetime. Since the cost to run the pump would be nominal, water bills would soon be a thing of the past. With this abundant source at my disposal, I could plant as many trees as I wished to take care of. At almost 3000 feet in elevation, I was in a good place for stone-seeded fruit trees such as apples, cherries and peaches if I could keep birds away from them. I envisioned an orchard in the desert, imagining myself in my golden years operating a fruit stand on Highway 62.

Deciding On Siding

Next I had to decide what I wanted for the exterior. I had intended to use fiberglass siding, a formulated mixture that is environmentally friendly and fireproof. The material is more expensive than wood, but since there had been a couple of fires near my area the year before, I felt it wise to give my structure added protection. I had several panels from one of the stores delivered. But when they arrived, my neighbor told me they'd be difficult to install. Like glass, they broke easily, and required special equipment, which he didn't own. He said I needed to find someone more experienced than he was with this material.

My search for someone else was not easy. None of the big box stores had fiberboard installers. Neither did small stores. Online, the manufacturer's website's nearest listing was three states away. I got a lead to a man nearby, but he was not available. The colleague he recommended never showed up and never cancelled. Looking around my neighborhood, I couldn't find any building with a fiberboard exterior. My contractor suggested "smart" plywood siding would add more strength to the cabin than this brittle material, and it was also treated with fire retardant. So I went with the plywood.

Delivery Blues

When I hear about delivery problems, it's usually a local deli sending the wrong sandwiches, or a pizza man with the wrong toppings. I assumed building supply places had better quality control and more experienced drivers than food establishments. Wrong!

I arranged a delivery the following week of plywood siding, drywall panels, and greenwall. The latter is a moisture and mold resistant variation of drywall suitable for bathrooms. To this I added an assortment of kitchen cabinets.

My contractor and his assistant were readying the place to be sided the day the driver arrived. Instead of sending out the usual bobtail truck, the store outsourced the delivery to a man who drove an eighteen-wheeler. Reluctant to travel on the dirt roads to my place, he parked two blocks away and insisted on forklifting the goods over. We encouraged him to drive his rig to my property as others had done before, but he refused.

A fifteen-minute unloading took over an hour. He dropped much of the siding and damaged many of the cabinets. To add insult to injury, he wouldn't take anything back. We had to return this ourselves, which delayed the project a full day and cost me extra time and money. With everything ready for the next day, the two men started early, finishing siding before sunset.

Inspired by drawings of the mixture of vertical and horizontal (lap) panels in the manufactured home brochures, I interwove these siding applications similarly. This added such a stylish pattern to the exterior that it continues to earn me compliments.

Drywall/Tape & Texture

Inside the cabin, stacks of drywall were waiting to be installed. The two workers covered the plumbing, wires, and insulation with these 4 by 8 foot sheets. The place was rife with the sounds of power saws and a special cut-out tool known as a sawzall, used to cut circles and other shapes to go around pipes, outlets, windows and doors. This was painstaking work, something I'd never have the patience or coordination to do. Their meticulous craftsmanship was often interrupted by mistakes and utterances of profanity. Fortunately, drywall is easily patched with mud and tape. When the drywall was in place, my cabin was no longer one room, but three.

An interior is not finished with drywall. Tape is necessary. Many people today, including my workers, recommend texture as well. I prefer the flat walls of yesteryear, but the craftsmanship needed for this seems to have gone the way of the typewriter and rotary phone. When I requested minimal texture, the men assured me they would keep it subtle. So far, they knew more than me what my cabin needed. They were right. When I arrived to see the result a few days later, I was pleased. They had given my place a touch of class.

Painting

I designated myself to be the painter. This step was critical to what followed. It preceded installing the kitchen cabinets, flooring, and appliances and had to be finished before the inspector would allow me to connect my house to the grid. A lot was riding on the paint job.

Painting is one of the few areas where I feel confident. Walls are my turf for two reasons. I like to try out a few shades of color before I choose the final ones. In my experience, paint chips are only an approximation and tend to look different than the final result. I also enjoy seeing my efforts materialize before my eyes. I bought small amounts of different shades of the peach color I saw in the Arizona factory tour. The lightest shade was for the kitchen, a medium tone for the living room and a more intense one for the bathroom. I had used this monochromatic approach elsewhere with excellent results.

My compulsive nature takes over when I paint and I hate to stop in midstream. However, I'm not always happy with my choices and need to tweak the coloring a bit lighter or darker until I am satisfied. We artistic types can drive ourselves crazy, making more work than necessary. After four full days of brushing and rolling, re-brushing and re-rolling, and re-re-rolling, my muscles were so sore I thought they'd given up the ghost. But I got the job done to my liking.

Cabinets And Countertops

I hoped the sandalwood cabinets and countertops I'd ordered would complement the peach walls. The living room was cluttered with their cartons, and when it was time to install them I was nervous. This was a $2,000 investment that, unlike paint, I wouldn't be able to change afterwards. My contractor and I unboxed one cabinet at a time, the upper wall cabinets first, the lower ones later. He carefully measured precise distances for each according to my design, hammering on the wall to find the studs for attachment. He drew nailing points on the wall and used a level to make sure the cabinets were flush with the walls, the ceiling, and themselves. I held them in place while he drilled and nailed. One false move and we'd have to start over. This work was intense, and the profanity profuse.

The pattern I'd designed started to emerge, and it looked great. Twice during this process, we opened a box to find a damaged cabinet, probably from that stubborn deliveryman. This required a trip to the store for replacement, causing more delay and expense. One of these bad finds turned out to be a blessing in disguise. When we opened the last of the cabinets, it had a lot of dings. Someone had returned the cabinet, and it was mistakenly sold as new. We couldn't return it until the next day. Overnight, I noticed its placement perpendicular to the wall blocked in the kitchen, spoiling the open feeling I'd intended. A test placement of the countertops proved this true. A smaller, shorter cabinet turned out much better. I take my hat off to design professionals who can see these things in advance (if they do). I can only imagine the nightmare and added expense that results when a designer or client demands a job be redone and restructured. Fortunately, in my case this was easily remedied.

Flooring

When these were finished, flooring was next. I considered vinyl squares, something I'd installed myself in my LA house. My workers advised I could do better. Though easy to put in, vinyl does not hold up well. Carpet was out of the question here in the desert, as sand is often tracked in. So I browsed the home improvement store tile, hardwood, bamboo and laminate flooring displays, comparing prices, colors, installation techniques, and reports of durability. For the bathroom, I chose ceramic tiles. For the living and kitchen areas, economy, upkeep, and ease of installation led me to laminate.

I picked out deep brown bathroom tiles and a light grout to offset it. My contractor's assistant happened to be an experienced tile man. He spent a day and a half cutting, shaping, and setting the tiles for this relatively small room. Even though this tile work set me back more than I expected, the result was excellent.

For the living room I chose laminate planks to blend with the cabinets and walls, buying acrylic sheets of underlayment to go between the flooring and the bottom surface. This material keeps the planks in place and provides cushioning much like carpet padding.

Before the flooring could be laid, I had to design a hearth area for the wood-burning stove and select material to set on top of it. At my neighbor's suggestion, I visited a quarry nearby that had three city blocks of choices. At this rock and stone Disneyland I took my dog along for a walk though seemingly endless piles. I was drawn to its many natural and cultured stones, each with patterns and streaks of color. She sniffed out her favorites. I jotted down the names of a few and got some price quotes. For her hard work, Stella was rewarded by one of the employees with some doggie treats.

Later, at a big box store I compared its selection with the quarry's. While the stone yard had more diversity, the store had an attractive Chinese slate in a blend of gray and peach at a good price. I bought a few boxes, choosing the best looking squares for the hearth.

When the hearth was framed, my neighbor put down the laminate planks, sawing and trimming them to fit around the hearth, cabinets, and closet. Once this painstaking piecing was done, the large planks went in quickly. By the end of the day, the cement slab was completely covered. Baseboard trim added a finishing touch.

Lighting

Next was a visit to the land of 1,001 light fixtures where I needed to choose for the kitchen, living room, and bathroom, and for the outside, a security sensor and address light. For the living room I browsed endless rows of ceiling fans. The selection was vast, and I enlisted a home improvement store guide. She flooded me with so many questions I could barely keep up. I was quizzed about blade and lamp size, real or faux wood, metal choice, wattage, etc. Paper or plastic is nothing compared to choosing brass, chrome, brushed nickel, white, rattan, contemporary, colonial, and tropical items. Prices ranged wildly from $50 to $500. The track lighting attraction had a similar obscene number of choices. I picked a brushed-nickel ceiling fan, which matched a brushed-nickel deco curved track light. I knew this bit of uptown might tempt my Morongo neighbors to tease me for being too Palm Springs. If my urban roots were showing, so be it.

Function dominated style for the other rooms. The kitchen kiosk revealed a large florescent fixture to flood the room with light, the lavatory lab, a modern overhead florescent circle. A light bulb strip over the medicine chest reminiscent of an actor's dressing room was not for me. A simple fixture with a chain sufficed for the closet.

The final exhibition was the exterior light extravaganza. Here, I chose midrange brass fixtures, nothing too pretentious shining on the jackrabbits and kangaroo rats to make them uncomfortable. For security lights, some rectangles complemented my windows. A simple address backlight completed this adventure.

Connecting To The Grid

In late July, I had gone to the Edison company offices to connect my cabin to the grid. I filled out the necessary paperwork, providing them with a copy of my grant deed and tax assessor's forms. When I asked how much it would cost, they said they wouldn't know until someone was sent out to assess the job. This was slated to happen in three weeks. More than two months went by before Edison did so. Even then, they wouldn't tell me the amount over the phone.

I'd heard stories of people paying ten, twenty thousand and more for this service. Nervously, I crept inside the office. After being hit with many extra charges elsewhere, I was expecting the worst. I was relieved to hear that two electric poles and a transformer would cost 11K. Then, even better news awaited. If I paid the entire amount, when anyone on my street later tapped into this equipment, I'd be given a couple thousand dollars refund for each new customer. Another option was to pay half the amount and forfeit any future refunds. I knew that most of the land near my parcel was bought up by a man with no interest in building anytime soon. I chose the half-price alternative. Fifty-five hundred was far less than I had expected.

I cut Edison a check and was told the work would be done within the month. One month turned into two. Although an installation date was set for the end of October, wildfires throughout Southern California forced the company to do repair work elsewhere. My job wasn't completed until November. It was a thrill at last to drive down my street and see huge electric poles and wires leading to the front of my property. But before I could get too excited about finally having electricity, an Edison employee told me they couldn't connect me to it until the inspector OK'd my building for occupancy.

When I talked to the inspector, he said I needed to complete a few things first. My water heater, appliances and electric wall heater would need to be in place, and my well would have to pass county tests for mineral and bacteria content. I checked the well driller to make sure he'd sent in his papers. He had, but said it would take a while for the government to respond. My neighbor recommended building an outside shed for the water heater before purchasing one, another postponement. The wall heater had to be ordered online, yet one more delay. I was making progress very slowly.

"The Pumpkin" Van

Planning logistics for moving my possessions to the cabin, I had the luxury of a long transition, not having to transport everything at once. Building my future house in segments, one fell swoop wouldn't be possible anyway. I decided to buy a truck or van to help carry things more conveniently. Another advantage of a second vehicle would be that I could park it next to the cabin when I wasn't there, making the place look lived in. Most rural houses have an old car or two parked in front, a common way of deterring potential burglars. Browsing the online classifieds, I didn't want anything new or expensive, hopefully under $2,000. I only needed an old clunker, one that would give me reliable transportation, even if its gas mileage was marginal.

In a copy of Truck Trader I saw an ad for a 1977 Dodge camper van at a low price of $1000. I took a car-savvy friend with me to investigate. It was a rusted burnt-orange color badly in need of a paint job. Although the owner didn't keep up its appearance, he maintained it in running condition. Incredibly tall, it appeared quite roomy inside and seemed to meet my needs. I offered $800, we settled at $900, and I drove it home the next day. Because of the color, I named it "The Pumpkin."

I put it to immediate use the next weekend hauling a wood stove to my cabin. However, when I stopped to pick up a large swamp cooler I'd ordered at a big store a month earlier, I found its cargo capacity was limited. Because there were so many built-ins inside, I couldn't fit the large cooler in the van without first taking it out of its carton. If I hadn't unpacked, I wouldn't have seen how dented it was until I'd driven all the way to the cabin. I was able to return the cooler right away for a refund. "The Pumpkin" was good luck. I was going to need more luck soon.

More Hoops

The cooler mishap added to my growing sense of frustration. Struggling to get everything done to turn on my utilities, I felt like a trained seal having to go through endless hoops. The inspector's requirements were not difficult to complete, but each took time. Although I was hoping to be ready by Thanksgiving, this wasn't likely.

Hoop #1 was the water heater shed. This task was made easier by the opening of a big box store nearby. No more sixty-mile round-trip drives to get materials. My neighbor picked up supplies there and built the shed in a day. Later we went back together and bought the water heater for the plumber to install. One less bell to answer! Hoop #2 was passed when the electric wall heater I ordered online arrived on my LA doorstep the next day. I brought it to the desert, and another bell soon rang its sweet tone.

When we made the final connections for the appliances, there were some snags. Stacking the washer and dryer was difficult, and the instructions were missing. I was unable to reach anyone at the store to solve the problem quickly. The kitchen sink facet leaked stubbornly until we figured that out. The stove and dishwasher were each so tight we had to carve niches into the cabinets to get them in. The bells ringing in my ears were now emitting a sour sound.

By the time the weekend was over, I was a nervous wreck. When it seemed I had satisfied the inspector's requirements, I made an appointment with him for what I hoped would be ready for occupancy approval. Tired and apprehensive, I drove The Pumpkin home, praying to get a little respite from my frustration to the desert. Little did I know, I'd encounter more trouble when I returned to LA.

Meanwhile, Back In The City

Back at my primary residence, the marbled joys of urban life were growing stale. Gridlock approached lockjaw on my commutes through town. It became rare to find a quick ride on the freeway during daylight hours. Stella and I became targets of harassment. Then, our illustrious mayor sent me a threatening letter.

One of the pleasures of residing in LA had been taking walks through our many parks. With Stella, these green zones became venues for her favorite game of fetch. In the part of town where I lived, these sparsely frequented areas had been forgiving when it came to canines. We had several favorite places for me to throw a ball, stick or Frisbee, and for her to run after to return with gusto. I carried a leash with me in case there were problems, but none ever occurred.

All at once, city officials decided to clamp down on freedom of dog owner expression. There had always been leash your pet signs, but they weren't enforced. Now, one park employee after another became a neo-Nazi canine killjoy. Most of them gave verbal warnings to leash her up. I'd snap on her choker until they left and then resume our fun. How can one play fetch on a leash?

I felt like a scofflaw watching out for "the man." Soon, written warnings were given. My name was put on a blacklist, and I was derisively told that a second violation would be an expensive citation. I was directed to the one dog park in the area, an ugly strip of worn out grass near smog-producing traffic. This doggie reservation, a poor excuse for a recreation area, seemed like something between the pogrom villages my great-grandparents had to endure in Eastern Europe and the trail of tears many Native Americans were forced to walk to their exiled wastelands. What a contrast to the wide-open spaces of my desert acreage.

Then something more egregious happened. After a very exhausting weekend, I accidentally left my sedan's headlights on when I parked in my garage. The next morning, the battery had run down and the car wouldn't start. Since I had the van, I drove it on my errands that day instead. I felt lucky to have not only two homes, but two vehicles as well. When I returned to my block, I noticed a police car dart around the corner. This was not a good sign. Getting closer, I saw the garage door was open. My car was gone.

Looking down the street, I witnessed my car and another one on the bed of a large tow truck. I ran after it yelling "thief," suspecting a new kind of urban crime. This brought quite a few neighbors out onto the street. One told me because my car alarm had sounded, the police had towed my car away. I was incredulous. They'd broken into my garage to take my vehicle. I knew it was going to cost a lot to get the car back. When I asked who had called the cops, no one admitted it.

Phoning my local precinct, I was told they had received a complaint. My car would soon be at the local impound yard. I drove my van there and paid $150 for the privilege of driving my own car back to my own house. If I had been there an hour later, the yard would have been closed, and the cost would have doubled. To add insult to injury, when I returned the garage door had been broken.

Calling the door company, I was told my warrantee didn't cover vandalism. I'd have to pay for any repair. I said it was the police broke the door, not a criminal. They didn't see any difference. Fortunately, the company sent the same repair guy who worked with me in the past. He fixed the door and didn't charge for the call.

This misbehaving garage door became a turning point for me once again. The unsupportive attitude of my neighbors, most new to the block, was telling. I had put up with numerous car alarms in the past. This event signaled me to move out of the area sooner, rather than later. My bond to the neighborhood was further broken.

A final straw arrived the next day in the form of a letter from our mayor requesting I pay the city a license fee for my home-based business. For 30 years, I'd been teaching music privately in my house. Now, hard up for cash, the city wanted me to pay for the privilege to continue to do so. I called the office and had the pleasure of telling them I was moving my business out of town.

Switching On The Power

Just when I was at the end of my patience, my contractor called to say we'd passed a provisional inspection, enough to allow Edison to install a meter and turn on my electricity. Though I'd made Thanksgiving plans in town, I spent the weekend afterwards at my cabin. It would be a pleasure to switch on the long awaited power.

The day after Thanksgiving, I loaded my sedan with personal items to set up my new household. Having spent the holiday with friends in town, I was in a thankful mood as I drove to the desert. When I arrived, my neighbor welcomed me warmly, showing me the new meter box, inviting me to turn on the breakers. He could have done this earlier, but wanted me to enjoy the dramatic moment. One of this book's photos captures this glorious event.

I went around the cabin, flipping on switches and testing out my new fixtures and appliances. The lights went on, the microwave beeped, and when I turned on the switch for the pump to send the water through my rehabbed residence, it was a thrill to turn the faucets and see H20 running through them. My neighbor also showed me how to set up the wood stove and fire it up with wads of newspaper, kindling and wood. I had numerous ends of unpainted lumber I could use until I got some genuine firewood.   Being that it was a cold day, we lit the stove right away. It worked like a charm.

All this joy was tempered by a few snafus. When we turned on the breaker for the electric wall heater, the thermostat shorted out and would not work. Even more upsetting was when the well's pressure relief valve flooded water onto the ground nearby. The pressure gauge went all the way to maximum. It did not shut off the pump as it was supposed to do. This was a threat to my plumbing and meant a delay in using my water right away. My plumber came over and we improvised a go-around, turning on the switch briefly to get water, but turning it off manually to stop the pump. I was advised to call the well guy immediately and use the pump as little as possible.

Another consideration was that since winter was approaching, I needed to get my cabin re-roofed. Much of its cover was worn out. My neighbor advised me to get this done before any winter rains, sparse as they are here, arrived. I set up an appointment the following week with a local roofer.

My Three-Room Haven

The workers departed, I left a message for the well installer and settled in for a day on my own. Now I was free to straighten up my place and decorate. The tub and sinks needed cleaning and I swept the floors of their construction dust. Next came putting up my art objects and arranging the furniture. The large tapestry I had bought in Prescott was the *piece de resistance*. When I hung it on the wall to the side of the stove, everything fell into place. My cabin was now a home, and a beautiful one at that.

By nightfall, it started to get cold, bone chilling cold. Having learned how to use the wood stove, I did the paper, kindling and lumber routine and soon had a vibrant fire going. It threw out so much heat I had to open a window a crack to cool the room down. Falling asleep in the very same futon bed I'd used for years, at first it seemed as if nothing had changed. Eerily familiar feelings arose, especially when I heard similar coyote howls as before. Then I'd open my eyes to this wonderfully decorated, insulated, and well heated room and had to pinch myself to see if I was a dreaming.

In the morning, even with the fire out, it was still warm inside. I threw some wood into the stove to keep it that way. In my new bathroom, I used all the functions one expects at home, things that up until then I had never experienced here. A toilet flush was miraculous, a hot shower even more transcendent. The water had a sulfur smell with which I am familiar from my visits to hot springs. A hot bath I took later that day in my new luxurious tub reaffirmed this. No more long distances were needed for this special treat. I could lounge in a health-inducing bath in my own residence.

The kitchen stove was not yet connected to propane, but the microwave was all I needed to fix an oatmeal and coffee breakfast. This three-room haven was all I'd hoped it would be and more. When the weekend was over, despite the cold weather, I delayed my to return to LA as long as possible.

The following week, I brought more belongings to Morongo, including wood blinds, a set of dishes, a clothes hamper, a spare television and a new stereo. Now I had privacy. The TV and radio were disappointing, as they did not pick up stations with clarity. My location nestled in the hills of this well-surrounded valley was not media friendly, at least until I got cable or satellite. However, playing CDs on my stereo didn't require reception, so I filled the cabin with the sounds of some of my favorite recordings. On a spare computer I was able to play a few games and do some writing.

A refrigerator I'd ordered a few days earlier was delivered the following day. Once I bought a few groceries, cooked a couple of meals, washed a few dishes, and relaxed comfortably, I felt at home. Ready to rearrange my schedule to spend as much time as possible living here, I could hardly wait to make this my permanent residence.

Just as I was getting comfortable, the weather became nasty, and, with little warning, a heavy rainstorm hit the area. This turned the dirt roads into large ponds and made transportation risky. It was good I had my food and toys as it became a long day and a half before the storm subsided. The following night, the temperature went below freezing, and I awoke to see ice all around the cabin and frozen water on the road and in the wash below. A howling chilly wind blew through the valley. Call it a dramatic welcome wagon or a baptism, this extreme weather was quite intense.

My neighbor came over to see how I fared. He pointed out an area in the kitchen ceiling where the water had leaked through the roof. Even the walls had watermarks. He urged me to move up the roofer's work if at all possible.

Later that day, warmer weather returned to melt the ice and allowed me to drive back to LA. I made a list of more supplies I needed. The week went by fast. Until my final inspection was passed, I didn't want to get complacent. Besides the roof, I needed to have a propane tank installed for my kitchen stove. The gas line for the tank was in place and the pressure gauge showed that everything was ready. However, I wasn't taking anything for granted.

Roofing

By the time I reached the roofer, he'd been flooded with calls. I wasn't surprised, since the area had received over two inches of rain, twice what had fallen over the entire year before. Many homes now needed his attention. Since I had booked him earlier, I hoped I'd be at the front of the line. He told me he could roof the house the next day. My relief was short-lived, because he called back to say the stores were out of roofing material. It would be a few more days before new supplies came in. I wasn't worried, as rains like we'd just experienced were rare here.

On the news, I heard that a new larger storm was expected the next weekend. My contractor was alarmed. He was disappointed to see the roofing hadn't been done, and concerned that much of our work could be threatened by additional leakage. I hadn't expected to visit the cabin that weekend, as I had a music event to attend in town. Seeing how important it would be to head off this threat, I drove out there to do some preventative maintenance.

At my contractor's suggestion, I bought some thick plastic sheeting made to protect roofs. I arrived just before sunset. We staple-gunned the material over the roof to keep it from being blown away in case it got windy. He was concerned that the plastic could become a huge kite if the wind got a hold of it. So we placed several large heavy pieces of lumber, some weighing almost 100 pounds, on top. It took an hour to get this done and we finished just as it got dark. I retreated to my cabin waiting for the oncoming storm.

My well-laid plans went awry. The night turned out to be more of a wind than rain event. Gale force gusts over sixty miles an hour raged most of the night. I was repeatedly awakened by the sounds of lumber rolling and crashing. I recoiled in my bed, afraid to see what damage had been done. Even Stella made strange doggie sounds in response to these menacing noises.

When dawn broke, I put on layers of clothing and walked out in the light freezing rain. The moisture had been minimal, but littered all around the cabin were piles of lumber, including many heavy pieces. Fortunately, none had caused any damage. Then a huge gust of wind blew half of the plastic off the roof into a huge kite. It had such force I was afraid the whole cabin would be blown away like in the Wizard Of Oz. I rushed to get a knife and cut off the staples that held the plastic down. This large sheet blew several hundred feet away onto the road in front of my property. I could see a traffic nightmare in the making. In the rain, I chased the plastic down and dragged it back to the side of the cabin, placing some of the lumber on top to hold it down. On the ground, it wasn't as much a flight threat as when it was aloft. I did the same thing with the other half.

The rest of the day saw similar winds, but no more rain. The next day, the winds died down. Just as I was getting ready to go back to LA, the roofer appeared with material and finally went to work. On the drive home, I had to make my way through intense thunderstorms, unbelievable traffic jams and many accidents on the highway. I found out later that the winds had returned, and the roofer couldn't finish the job until a couple of days afterwards. My "Little Home On the Prairie" movie wasn't anywhere as romantic as I'd expected. As if this weren't enough, Mother Nature presented me with another weather challenge a few days later.   Before I could get my propane tank installed, I had another emergency to deal with.

Frozen Pipes

The next weekend a brand new roof awaited me. With another rainstorm on its way, I was relieved. This time, both precipitation and wind were light. Most of the threatening clouds stayed west of the mountain ranges, only occasional moisture passed through to the desert. From my vantage point, I could see the progress and regress of the storm. Typically, after one of these Pacific cold fronts blows by, the clouds clear and the temperatures plummet for a night or two. Sure enough, the mercury dipped into the twenties.

Inside my warm sanctuary I didn't mind. One morning, when I woke early, I decided to use my brand new front-loading washer for the first time. Filling the machine with dirty laundry and putting detergent in the appointed slot, I pushed the "on button." Nothing happened. No water rushed in to fill the washer. I was crestfallen.

Testing my kitchen faucet to see if the water to my house was on, the same thing happened. No water. Outside, the thermometer read 28 degrees. Putting two and two together, I wondered if my water supply had frozen in the night. Never having experienced anything like this before, I hoped that when the sun rose over the eastern hills, this situation would resolve itself.

When the sun's rays warmed up the soil, everything returned to normal. My washer worked fine. I checked the pressure on the well pump. It was over the 50 psi limit, not a good sign. When I told my neighbor, he was surprised. His place fifty feet higher in elevation than mine didn't go below freezing. It seemed that my lower location sat in a cold zone, and I had to protect the pipes.

The even colder months of January and February were approaching, and I needed to insulate my water supply before then. My neighbor recommended laying a few rolls of Styrofoam insulation around the pipes, fastening them with duct tape. I did what he advised as best as I could before returning to LA. When he assessed my work, he said I hadn't done an adequate job. Every inch had to be covered completely. This was a temporary fix. I had to leave right away for LA and return home with unfinished business on my mind.

Christmas week came and went without my ability to finish this job since I wanted to stay in town with friends for the holidays. I had some health problems, which prevented me from driving to my cabin for a quick overnight fix. It wasn't until a couple of weeks later that I was able to get back.

The weather report warned that the nights in the desert would soon again go below freezing. I was concerned, hoping I'd given my pipes enough insulation. On my next visit, I returned with the right stuff and spent a few hours winding feet of heavy tape around each pipe and fixture, covering them with styrofoam. Once this was done, I wrapped additional duct tape over my work to lock this in. I no longer had to worry about frozen pipes. Only one final hoop remained before the final inspection, the propane tank.

Propane Tank

My next task was to find a propane company to install a tank. This also had its learning curve. I shopped online for companies that handled propane in my area. One was an outfit my neighbor had hired for his house and two others were nearby. The company my neighbor had used was open that weekend. The woman behind the desk handed me a stack of papers for me to read before applying for delivery. This included a detailed brochure warning me about the dangers of propane and a multi-page contract with a lot of fine print. A credit history form was also included. She said I'd need to sign these papers and bring a deposit of $350 before she'd even talk to me. I was put off by her attitude and all the paperwork.

On Monday I called company #2. A girl with a friendly voice said she could take all my information over the phone and schedule an appointment for delivery. They only needed a $250 deposit, which could be paid after the tank was delivered and set up. I decided to look no further and we set a date for installation.

I waited at my cabin with baited breath. I was looking forward to using my brand new stove and say goodbye to my primitive Coleman burner, praying there would not be any further complications. Soon a large gas truck appeared a few blocks away on one of the dirt roads leading up to my place. The driver went extremely slowly, prolonging my anticipation. When he got out of his truck, my dog Stella rushed up to him with a stick, which he threw several times for her to fetch. He was as friendly as the receptionist.

I was surprised when the man pulled out a crane and lifted a huge tank onto the ground next to my meter. I'd been expecting a tank half its size. He said this was the one ordered. I laughed and told him my needs were modest, only one appliance. He replied that it wouldn't cost me any more plus it would give me room to grow. After putting wooden shims under the tank and leveling it out, he went inside my cabin to test the stove. Everything worked perfectly. He gave me a small brochure explaining the characteristics of propane and its safe usage. Taking my check, he gave me a receipt and left. I immediately called building and safety to set up my final inspection.

The Final Inspection

With all the drama I'd been through since Thanksgiving, the last inspection was a breeze. A lingering problem with the electric heater was remedied with a new thermostat. The new roof was in place, the wood stove and appliances all worked. I held my breath when the inspector arrived. He gave the place a once over, complimenting me on the good job I'd done. He signed a few papers, shook my hand and went on his way. No trumpets, no fanfare, and no celebration.

Finally, I had no more deadlines. I resolved to take a couple of months break from construction and enjoy my new rehabbed home as it was. And, as it is said in the Old Testament, I rested after all my hard work and decided that it was good. I hoped and prayed that the construction of the two new rooms would be much easier.

On a lonely selection far out in the West
An old woman works all the day without rest,
And she croons, as she toils 'neath the sky's glassy dome,
`Sure I'll keep the old place till the childer come home.'
She mends all the fences, she grubs, and she ploughs,
She drives the old horse and she milks all the cows,
And she sings to herself as she thatches the stack,
Sure I'll keep the old place till the childer come back.'

Henry Lawson

Three-Room Haven

Address light installed

Kitchen before appliances

Finished kitchen

Finished bathroom

Finished living room

Finished bedroom/living room

Finished three-room cabin

Switching on the power

ADDING TWO NEW ROOMS
A Break From Construction

It is a Biblical maxim that the Almighty created for six days and rested on the seventh. I'd been building for six months straight and desperately needed to follow His example. For the next month I took a well-deserved break from construction. This period of cold weather and short days wasn't well suited for building. Instead, I took the time to adjust to living in my new desert home, which was a pleasure. Everything worked well and was very easy to maintain.

Even though Morongo Valley winters are usually much chillier than LA, the new house was so well insulated with double-pane windows and weather-stripped doors it was easier to keep warm than my old Craftsman style residence in town. Being that this year was a cold winter by California standards, it was ironic that I was actually more comfortable in my desert abode.

During the break, I was able to further explore my new community. Shopping in nearby Yucca Valley was very convenient, and Palm Springs was more accessible than I had expected with hardly any traffic. Twenty miles in LA can sometimes take an eternity, but here it was a snap. Despite the extreme weather, the more time I spent in Morongo Valley, the more I liked it. When February arrived, the weather warmed a bit, and the sun set later each day. With my energy renewed, it seemed a good time to start the ball rolling and begin adding the two new rooms I had planned.

Permit #2

Having learned from my earlier trials, I was able to handle things more easily. Once again, I had to seek government permission to build. This was a relative piece of cake, albeit a $250 slice. No porta-potties were needed this time, no generators, no additional plumbing, no utility hook-ups, and no new people to hire. This round seemed to be a simpler undertaking.

The lady at Building and Safety took my check and hooked me up with the same friendly inspector. She gave me a yellow-lined paper form on which he could initial his approvals. There would be less for him to sign off on. Though there were fewer hoops to go through, I did have to deal with some new requirements. The roof over the existing patio was not built to code and had to be torn down. The outdoor slab needed to be modified and fortified, since it was built with a drainage tilt, and indoor foundations have to be level. Cement footings were required for further strength.

Clearing The Construction Site

Before I could start building, I needed to clear the construction site. I removed piles of cartons, lumber, drywall, roofing material, pipes and other debris lining both sides of the cabin. For several weeks I filled one heavy-duty black construction bag after another with an enormous amount of material. I'd break up much of this into smaller pieces, then bag and stuff them into my camper van. Since I was allowed only one visit a week at the Morongo dump, I was grateful to have a large enough vehicle to transport a lot of trash at once. Little by little, my property started looking attractive again. I was getting so much exercise I lost weight and built up some muscles.

The visits to the dump were a favorite activity for Stella. She'd run around the dumpsters, sniff the trash, and make friends in the process. My pooch became a favorite of the guy who ran the place. The way he whistled at her, whenever we'd get near the yard, her tail would begin wagging vigorously. Too bad he didn't like her enough to let me dump trash there twice a week.

Urban Plumbing Woes

In the meantime, I had to deal with some plumbing problems in LA. I knew I'd need some infrastructure rebuilt before I could put my home on the market, but had postponed it. By mid-January, the galvanized pipes under the house became so constricted that some of the faucets barely had any water pressure. Then a pipe burst pipe and had to be fixed right away. The bathroom needed a new sub-floor and up-to-date fixtures. It seemed the right time to do all of this at once.

That week, I ran into a plumber friend who complained that with the economy in bad shape, he really needed work. When I offered him the job, he agreed to start the next day. Since he'd have to tear apart the bathroom, I gave him the OK to upgrade it all. He said he'd do this in three days for about $2.000. It seemed to be a good deal.

The damage was worse than we thought. Two days into the job he got hired to do a big project somewhere else. He could only work on occasional weekends and the project progressed slowly. Three days turned into six weeks. For over a month, all I had for a bathroom was a working toilet and no sink or shower. The job doubled in price when more complications arose. In the middle of this disruption, I had already made plans to start new construction in the desert. I wound up commuting between two construction zones, something I never want to experience again.

Back To The Drawing Board

Meanwhile, I firmed up my designs for the two new rooms, trying to make these additions as trouble free as possible. For the slab, I chose to put a cement footing under the north and south sides and extend it to the west. The pass-through from the kitchen to the dining area would enable me to serve meals there easier and serve as a gateway to the outdoor patio. My manufactured home-cabin combo had a separate room for music. Now, I needed to incorporate this function into the bedroom. Between the two projected new spaces, I sketched a large closet area with built-ins to house clothes, dresser drawers and` business file storage. A sliding glass door would open to a separate patio. Compared to the cabin rehab, this undertaking was much simpler.

When my contractor and his assistant were ready to do the required roof teardown, I wasn't able to be there. I was finishing my bathroom in LA. Disassembling the overhang, columns and pillars, they placed the lumber neatly in a pile for reuse. The roof itself was not recyclable, so its remnants wound up scattered by the side of the house. More trips to the dump awaited my burgeoning muscles.

When I next visited the cabin, it was a shock to see it back in its original size.   The 400 square-foot structure seemed tiny.   However, the unobstructed view was even more beautiful.

Re-slabbing

The next step was to build the frames for the new slab. A series of storms put this on hold. People say it never rains in Southern California, especially in the desert. This year was the exception to prove the rule. The downside was a week's delay. An upside was the appearance of beautiful snowcaps on the mountains to the west. We even got a dusting of snow in Morongo. Another blessing was the greening of the landscape. Short grass-like plants carpeted the area. Spring looked to be filled with large displays of wildflowers.

Finally, the stormy weather subsided. The new slab was ready to be built above the original one. We hired a cement truck to bring its gray goop for the foundation of the new rooms. I was still busy in LA when my contractor called to say he'd finished the slab frame and I needed to be there to give a check to the cement pourer.

I arrived late the following night a few hours before this event was to take place. I was rudely awakened at 6:30 the next morning by a phone call. It was my contractor barking at me to get up immediately and help him with some last minute set up before the concrete man arrived. I hated waking up so early, and needed to put toothpicks in my eyes to prop them open. Even coffee hardly helped to give me a jump-start. What brought me to my senses was the arrival of the cement truck, a large colorful, noisy piece of machinery. Grabbing a camera, I got ready to document the dramatic moment. Stella had to be locked inside the house, since dogs and wet cement are a bad mix. As the truck parked on one side of the cabin, my neighbor and his assistant put on high rubber boots and gathered a few tools to level the viscous stuff when it was ready to come down the chute.

What followed made excellent choreography. The truck driver released dark gray gravelly mixture into the frame one area at a time as the two men waded in to spread it around with their shovels and rakes. They waved to the driver to move back and forth until one half of the slab was filled. They rough-leveled this with a huge piece of lumber. Then the truck drove around to the other side to repeat the procedure for the other half. When the frame was filled, they signaled for him to stop. I handed the driver a check for a few hundred dollars and watched him drive off.

The men worked quickly to fine-tune what had been a rough mix only minutes earlier. They made their work look like frosting a cake, like boys playing in the mud. However, it was exacting, painstaking labor. They continued to use finer tools to make adjustments. Within a half-hour the new slab was as smooth as glass.

I could hear Stella pacing back and forth inside wanting to be part of all this activity, but there was no way she could be included. It would be a few hours before the cement would be firm enough to resist her paw prints. The workers advised me to spray a fine mist of water on the slab every couple of hours that day to help it set. By sunset, the new foundation was ready.

More City Blues

March roared in as expected, not with rain, but with winds. Little did I know when I returned to LA, winds of change would be there too, crooning the blues like the singer Howlin' Wolf himself.

When I got back home late one morning, Stella jumped out of my car for her customary sniff of the garden across the street. A few hours later someone posted a hastily scrawled signed in large capital letters to leash my dog or they would call the police. This came without any previous warning. Since my neighbors seemed to like my dog, I was quite surprised. Then I remembered that a middle-aged woman who rented a room nearby had been giving me surly looks lately. She'd never said a word, so I had no idea what was bugging her. The next day when an unleashed Stella followed me to my car, this poor excuse for a human being yelled that this was the last straw. She was calling the cops. I was so angry I told her to go ahead and be an a-hole if she wanted to. My dog is hardly ever unfriendly. And I am rarely profane.

I realized shortly after this altercation that since Stella is a pit bull, as her owner, I might be legally vulnerable. Not liking to cause rifts with anyone, I tried to nip this in the bud. I wrote a nice note to this busybody, saying that out of respect for her, in the future I would keep Stella on a leash to and from my car. I added she didn't have to go to such lengths to get her wish. A simple request would have sufficed. I inserted it in her mailbox, hoping to put the matter to rest.

A few days later I received several letters, all with our mayor's name on the letterhead. The animal shelter had received a complaint my dog was on the street unleashed, an infraction. They required me to show up at a court hearing with a certificate of neutering, rabies shots, and a dog license. This was the third notice from the city in three months. I began to see a pattern of harassment. At least this time I knew who the perpetrator was.

I wasn't able to deal with this right away, as I was needed then in the desert. The delay allowed me to cool down and take care of things later with more detachment. I had the necessary paperwork and found I could pre-empt the court date by coming into the shelter with my certificates. My vet had written on the forms that Stella was a Labrador mix to cover me in case of any hassles. She is as much a lab as I am Chinese, but no matter. When I showed up, all I had to pay was $15 for a license tag. The people there had fun with Stella's name when I told them it came from the Marlon Brando movie.

Other legal notices included rate hikes for utilities and trash pickup plus a summons to serve on jury duty, a hardship for me since I was so buried in construction. Filing for an extension, I now had several more reasons to leave LA sooner rather than later.

Framing, Shopping & Wiring #2

While I was taking on LA's canine and human legal systems, my contractor was ready to frame the walls for the new rooms. I fielded quite a few calls from him that week. He'd placed an order for lumber and other materials from a new company to be delivered pending my credit card payment over the phone. I complied.

By the time I returned to the cabin, he and his assistant had finished the wall frames and were busy hammering on the rafters for the ceiling and roof. Soon, I had a fully enclosed space, albeit windowless. The house was growing by leaps and bounds, happening so fast I couldn't believe it. That day, I visited the local big box store to select windows and doors, a task by then I was familiar with. Because these west-facing rooms bore the brunt of the afternoon sun, I spent extra for high-efficiency low-emission glass.

A couple of days later, Highway 62 housed a caravan to the home improvement store for a shopping spree. Our procession included the two builders, the electrician, and myself (plus Stella). We formed our own parade in a large pick-up truck, a cargo van, an SUV, and my little black Mazda. At the store, each of us (sans Stella) grabbed a platform and piled it high with drywall, lumber, windows, doors, insulation, wires, hardware, light fixtures and more. We made a conga line at the contractor's register. I forked over more than $3,000 in one fell swipe of my orange-colored credit card. All four vehicles were crammed full with supplies, hopefully enough to finish the rooms. Shortly after unloading, I left for work in LA knowing that I was in good hands.

By the time I returned to the cabin, the construction had progressed with the windows and sliding glass door in place. The electrician arrived and started drilling holes in the studs and lacing them with wires for the lighting, ceiling fans, and outlets. Outside the cabin, he installed a sub-panel to handle the extra load I'd need for my computer and music gear. He added a few can lights that I could adjust for specific lighting requirements. Things were going so quickly and smoothly, we were soon ready for insulation and drywall.

More Delays

After such a productive spurt, it was inevitable something would slow the project down. Sure enough, more delays ensued. The next inspection was not the usual snap. Building and Safety was overbooked. Our inspector was not available, so he sent a young man, new to the job, to look things over. I imagine this guy felt he needed to assert his authority. He forced us to postpone working on the walls until a roof was installed. So much for speed.

The roofer was busy and couldn't help us right away. Then, as fate would have it, the weather report predicted rain that weekend. Since we wanted to roof the place as soon as possible, my workers volunteered to do it themselves. In the interim, we needed a layer of plastic sheeting for protection. This required several hours of staple-gunning and weighing down the material. Another trip to the home improvement store for roofing material and adhesive was called for. Though the rain never fell, a cold spell made roofing untenable. We had to wait for the weather to warm for the adhesive to take hold.

A week later when the roof was finally done, we called the inspector for approval. We learned from him that we could have constructed the walls all that time, even without a roof. In the meantime, my neighbor had made plans for a short vacation and his assistant had found other work. Construction was halted yet again.

My usual optimism was being sorely tested. Compounding these disappointments was the sub-prime mortgage crunch, a downturn in the housing market, rising unemployment, and a depressing economic outlook. Many of my private students began canceling or cutting back their music lessons. Some quit studying entirely. A class I was scheduled to teach at a state university was dropped due to budget cuts. Teachers were given pink slips all over the state. The whole country seemed to be going into the red. Gasoline and food prices were escalating through the roof.

I hated turning on the news. All of it was bad. My income and home equity each were dropping every week. I wanted to finish construction, move to the desert, and put my home on the market before prices fell even further. Waiting to resume building was a nail biting experience.

Walls, Mud And Paint

A large pile of drywall panels lay in the middle of the dining room for the longest time. When my neighbor was ready to build again, he nailed each panel onto the frames, cutting pieces as needed. Adding mud and texture gave the rooms a finished appearance.

I put on my painting clothes and immediately went to work with rollers and brushes in hand. I applied a light peach color to the bedroom and a light green to the dining room. These natural hues reflected the landscape outside. Painting furiously, I brought my muscles to familiar points of exhaustion. It was a dirty job, but I was the only one whose rates were within my budget. When finished, I threw the ball back to my neighbor so he could install the flooring.

Floors, Closets And Storage

Rather than spend more for fancy flooring, I decided to use the same wood laminate material as in the renovated cabin. Contrasting throw rugs to differentiate the spaces could come later. The main challenge was linking the living and dining areas. This required precision cuts to ensure continuity. My contractor put underlayment over the slab, placing the flooring pieces on top, fastening each tongue-and-groove style. The completed job looked great.

With the flooring in place, we installed a closet organizing kit I had purchased, starting with two large towers, adding several drawers with exterior doors. On one side, shelves with heavy brackets lined the wall, and on the other, two rods served for hanging clothes. Within an eight feet width of closet space, I had enough to handle my needs. Using this built-in structure meant I didn't have to buy bedroom furniture, leaving room for my music equipment.

We finished both rooms with baseboards at the junction of the walls and floor. Once again, the spaces looked finished. All we had left to do was put in the air conditioning.

Air Conditioning

The approaching summer months would soon be crying out for mitigation. Most desert people recommend swamp coolers to beat the heat, and I had expected to use one. I'd always been told that they use far less electricity than a/c units. Swamps inject moist air into a room while conditioners blow in machine cooled air. The only downside I was warned about was that in moist monsoon weather they don't work well, as the air is already too wet.

A swamp was not a good choice for my bedroom since the electric equipment I planned to use there required dry air. There were no swamp coolers available in the stores, so we installed the bedroom a/c first. I was surprised at how effective this appliance was. It put out an amazing amount of cooling with a powerful fan that brought the temperature down very quickly. When I took advantage of the energy saver option, the amount of electricity used was very little.

When we went to the home improvement store a couple of weeks later to pick up a swamp cooler for the living room, the aisles were crammed full of these machines. Compared to the svelte air conditioner, they were huge, unwieldy, and frankly, ugly. It took a lot of effort just to transport one to the cabin. Installing this humongous contraption looked to be a major job.

My contractor and I faced each other with trepidation. He suggested we scrap the project and return the darn thing. His arguments were convincing. Swamp coolers need a lot of maintenance. Parts have to be replaced and there is standing water that gathers bacteria and needs cleaning. What savings there might be in energy costs would be offset in replacement parts. The a/c unit was low maintenance. I didn't need any arm-twisting. We returned the cooler and bought a room a/c like the one in the bedroom. With these units both in place, I was well equipped to deal with the oncoming summer heat.

Opening Up The Rooms

Before we set up arrangements for the inspector to give us a final approval, I wanted to make a couple of changes to open up the rooms. The first was to remove the original front door to my old cabin, which up to this point separated the living and dining areas. Suddenly, the old boxy look was replaced with a modern spacious feel with more light and cross-ventilation. The living room opened to an alcove, a perfect place to put in some bookshelves. My modest-sized house immediately looked brighter and larger. An equally effective improvement was creating the pass-through to the dining room. This opened up both areas. An added bonus was that I could now look out from the kitchen and see the mountain vista through the dining room window.

The final inspection only took a few minutes. After he signed off on the house, the inspector complimented our work. With everything in place, it was now time to start moving in my belongings. I could hardly wait.

Moving My Stuff To Morongo

I don't know which is worse, moving all at once or in installments. A one-shot approach can be rough. This often had been a week of intense packing, fighting the temptation to reminisce over items from the past, usually followed by a nail-biting day watching moving professionals transport my things to the new residence. An expensive bill was paid, and I was left with the task of unpacking and setting up. However, a few days later I'd be back on my feet and functioning.

This time, I thought I was fortunate to be able to move leisurely without the pressure of deadlines. It turned out to be more like Chinese water torture. The task went on and on. I'd lived in my house over twenty years, and though not a pack rat, I still managed to accumulate a lot of stuff, both personal and business. Since I was moving to a smaller home, much of this needed to be discarded or given away. Though I don't consider myself to be an especially sentimental person, this was a draining, emotional experience.

I may have saved on mover's fees, but I had to load up my car over a dozen times. For some of the large bulky items I rented a cargo van. Starting the moving process in April, it wasn't until June that my belongings were able to say adios to Nuestra Senora La Reina De La Ciudad De Los Angeles.

The Transport Of Ebenezer Von Kitty

Midway in this moving process, I needed to transport my cat Ebenezer Von Kitty, or Ebner as I call him, to our new home. With mixed tabby and Siamese lineage, Ebenezer has smarts, personality and paranoia in copious quantities. Seeing our furniture and belongings disappear bit by bit, he knew what was up and didn't like it. In contrast to my dog Stella who loves to improvise, Ebner is a creature of habit and resisted change strongly. This adorable but stubborn feline spent almost his entire 9 years of age in the same residence and was not going to give up his territory without a fight.

I always had difficulty taking him in the car to the vet, needing to resort to sedating him with pills. For this move, I gave him a double dose mixed into his favorite meal of canned tuna. Although drugged, he still fought tooth, claw and nail. It was a major effort to get him inside his cardboard cat carrier. Even after I did, he carved a hole in it and escaped. I had to go to the pet store and buy a steel cage for the occasion. It took a desperate lunge to grab him and lock him inside. I had scratches all over my arms for days as a result.

He meowed loudly the entire ride to Morongo, driving Stella and me crazy. Yet, it only took a few minutes in the new house for him to calm down and get adjusted. Once he did, this half-tabby aristocat took immediate possession of the residence. Soon he was rubbing his body against my leg and giving orders for food and petting just like old times.

My Five-Room Haven Interrupted

As I approached the end of this transfer period, my piano, my dining table and a new sofa bed were comfortably situated in the dining room. I hung up some wall art, had a meal on my table, and spent my first night in this new room. The bedroom was out of the question, filled to the brim with boxes to be sorted out later on. After a long day I collapsed into the sofa bed. Before long, my familiar dog-on-one-side, cat-on-the-other side formation fell into place. This truly was a comfort. I woke up in a light green room with my pets and belongings surrounding me. In this five-room haven, life began returning to normal at long last. After all this time, work and expense, I was grateful to have these rooms completed with indoor plumbing, electricity, new appliances, heating, air conditioning, custom decorated walls, and my creatures and comforts intact.

This serenity was short-lived. I was looking forward to finishing the outside of the house with landscaping, a utility room, and outdoor patio areas. But suddenly I needed to put these projects on hold. More work and more pressure soon clamored for my attention.

At the beginning of May, I had casually started shopping for a real estate agent to help me sell my LA home. I contacted a local company, the same one I'd used when purchasing the house over twenty years before. The woman who headed the outfit remembered the residence and its layout after all these years. She was very professional, personable, and knowledgeable. She took an immediate interest in the property. Her son, an able assistant and third generation from a family of realtors, was equally involved. I knew at once that they were the right people to represent me.

She had both words of encouragement and a stern warning for me. Because my home was on a hilltop, it was well situated for selling. This area was in demand as few single-family homes were on the market at the time. However, lending institutions were starting to have foreclosure problems with houses nearby. The explosion of financially distressed homes dominating the outskirts of LA was spreading to inner metropolitan neighborhoods like mine. The competition would soon be fierce. She said if I wanted to get decent money for the house, I had to have it ready to sell right away. This meant a delay to further improvements in the desert. My full attention and budget needed to be focused in LA immediately.

I spent the following few weeks furiously modernizing the house, with the help of my contractor neighbor who traveled there to assist me. We worked in a spurt of activity installing a new kitchen, replacing several doors and windows, and repaired substandard outlets and fixtures. I hired other workers to re-roof and re-carpet a fair amount of the house. While they toiled, I painted the outside and inside of the residence myself. My contractor tore down the old rotting deck over my garage and built a snazzy new one as an extension of my front porch. All this resulted in quite a dramatic makeover.

To say I labored many 12-hour days during this period is not an exaggeration. I spent $15,000 above and beyond the plumbing and bathroom upgrades earlier in the year to make my place competitive in a buyer's market. By mid-June, we barely finished in time for a scheduled open house. I literally experienced my own version of the TV series "Flip This House".   Anxious and exhausted, I felt like many of the home sellers on the Home And Garden cable TV station.

We had several open houses. All were well attended and there were a few interested buyers. But with the real estate market in freefall, no one came through with an immediate offer. Not only were prices falling, mortgage loans were getting hard to obtain. Despite my best efforts to get on the market in time, I was too late to escape the housing crisis. There was nothing else for me to do but reduce my expectations, lower the price, and retreat to my desert home. Hopefully, the right buyer with his or her financial ducks in a row would eventually fall in love with the house and make an offer. In the meantime, I focused once again on my Morongo Valley property.

Landscaping

Springtime is the best time to set out new plants in the desert, after the last frost and before summer's intense heat. It is also the best time to buy trees and shrubs, as nurseries stock up for the onslaught of do-it-yourself gardeners like me. Years previously I had made a good start with my dozen trees. Midway through the construction of the two new rooms, when the weather warmed enough to start working in my front yard, I added to this. In April I planted several more trees, established a hedge along the road in front of my property, and set decorative plants in the slightly hilly area between the road and the level pad in front of the house. Although I intended to keep much of my two-and-a-half acre parcel in its natural state, I had a lot of space to play landscape architect.

Because of the area's extreme climate, only specimens hardy enough to stand both hot and cold temperatures were feasible. In this sandy soil and dry climate, frequent irrigation is necessary, and drought resistant plants are a must. Morongo Valley is in a wind zone, and all specimens need to withstand regular onslaughts of strong breezes. The land is overrun with jackrabbits and kangaroo rats whose appetite for flora is a constant nuisance. I learned this early on when I planted some beautiful yellow flowering shrubs in my first year that got gobbled up immediately. Even my trees had to have protective screening to keep critters at bay.

For the front hedge I planted a row of oleanders. I never was a big fan of these shrubs, but because of their poisonous nature, animals leave them alone. There were many colors of oleander flowers in the nurseries, very different from the common white and pink ones bordering countless California highways. I found bright red, yellow, salmon and peach blooms. Once established, they are very low maintenance, and they grew quickly and blossomed profusely.

To give the place a mountain feel, I added a row of blue point junipers. Most desert gardeners use Italian cypress with their tall, vertical leaves, but I find them too formal. The blue points have an attractive blue-green color and a broader base. Junipers are not supposed to be rabbit food, but I had to put protective screens around them once the jacks in the area started dining chez moi.

A row of multi-colored bougainvilleas went in next. These hardy drought and heat-resistant plants have abundant brilliant flowers ubiquitous in California gardens. Usually grown as climbing vines on fences or trellises, they adapt well as shrubs, something I observed many homes in the Palm Springs area. I tried the shrub approach with some success. Their thorns are supposed to deter rabbits, but I needed to envelop them with protection as well. Directly in front of my house I planted a few cactuses and an ocotillo. Although they grow fairly slowly, I made an investment for several years hence instead of trying to get immediate results.

On the southern end of the house I added a couple of pepper trees and another eucalyptus. I had planned to put in drip irrigation to take care of these, but I wound up making a habit of taking a hose and watering each one individually. This became such a pleasant task, like nurturing and feeding my pets, I kept it as one of my new rituals.

For the west side of the house, I hired a grading professional with a huge tractor to level out the hilly area and extend the yard. He carted load after load from the dry wash below and deposited them inside a retaining wall my contractor and I had built the week before.

To the north I started a small grove of fruit trees. With all the talk of global warming, it was a good feeling to know I'd be making a contribution to mitigating the greenhouse effect on our planet. Besides oxygenating my humble place in the sun, someday I might even realize my vision of a fruit stand on Highway 62.

Utility Room

One of the important last additions to my home was a utility room. The shed for the water heater on the north side of the original cabin had a lot of wasted space around it. A larger structure could house the heater and my washer and dryer as well. I designed a twelve-by-eight area to combine these functions. It would also create space for shelves and storage. I was going to build the utility room separate from the house, but my contractor suggested that it be an extension of the residence, a great idea. Besides the added strength of this approach, it made the house appear to be much wider.

We poured a small cement slab for the addition, and while we were at it, set another foundation for an outdoor patio. This went much like before. The frames were built, the cement truck arrived to dump its mixture down the chute, and the two workers smoothed the area out. It was a gray, gooey success. A few days later, when the cement was completely dry, we framed the utility room. Fascia boards integrated this with the main building.

The next day we connected the frames with OSB and sided the walls. Being an outside room, insulation and drywall were not needed. The windows and door were installed next. When I painted the exterior with the colors of the main residence, no one could tell this was an add-on.

Patio And Yard Space

The final construction job was building the patio over the porch slab, surrounding it with yard space. I purposely left an area between the utility room and the new patio un-cemented for a semi-shaded garden.

My contractor and I designed a two-prong overhang to designate the two contrasting patio areas. The new covering required both solid and slatted construction.

At our local home improvement center, the employees had gotten to know us so well they began teasing us for being junkies who needed our weekly fix. It began to feel like that. We selected the necessary lumber and hardware plus cement for the posts as well as several gallons of primer and glossy white paint. Once we got back to the house, we assembled well over one hundred pieces of lumber in a neat pile for my paint preparation task.

I won't describe the pleasures of placing one piece of wood after another onto a couple of sawhorses and administering three coats of paint on each in the blistering one hundred degree summer heat. I won't elaborate on the numerous "seven pieces of wood, only ninety-three more to go" countdowns I made during this time. I won't repeat the countless expressions of profanity that escaped my lips in the ensuing hours or confess how many gallons of lemonade and cold beverages I consumed daily to help me get through this. I won't even mention the countless Epsom salt baths I needed afterwards to soothe my aching muscles. Oops, I did. Sorry!

I could have hired someone else for this, but my budget was near its limit. Besides, this gave me the right to complain, one of the great pleasures of life for someone from my ethnic background, almost as rewarding as bakery bargaining. When I was done, it was my turn to hear my contractor shout profanities of his own as he installed the roof in the summer heat. After my latest ordeal I was oozing with empathy for him. As neither of us were spring chickens, we were entitled to our streams of verbal grievance.

Blood, sweat, tears and a depleted pocketbook soon bore fruit. In a few days there was a glorious new patio overhang painted in sparkling bright white. I moved the patio furniture from the living room to its proper location. Instantly, I had a great outdoor dining area and a more spacious living room. The slotted pieces of wood over the semi-shaded garden looked very stylish.

Just as I thought my task was done and my muscles could recover, my contractor came up with yet another good suggestion, a veritable "West Side Story". Why not build a similar overhang on the west side of the house above the recently created back yard. This would provide additional shade and make the two west-facing rooms a lot cooler. The project would give me a lot of bang for my buck. After yet another building material store junket, I endured two more days of paint preparation stress. This new and thankfully last construction job soon became another welcome addition.

The Final Push

I was looking forward to finishing this last project, collapsing into a sofa bed and retreating from the world. This reverie was interrupted when my realtor called with news of a buyer for my LA house. The last price reduction had done the trick. We had multiple offers. My Houdini of an agent had pulled a rabbit out of a hat, playing one buyer against the others. This resulted in a bid over the asking price. What a coup, especially in that challenging economy!

Now that I was going into escrow, all unfinished business had to be completed right away. The eaves' peeling paint needed to be scraped off and reapplied before the inspector arrived. Though thrilled about selling my home, I was all painted out. However, the news buoyed my spirits, and I made one final push. I could always fall into my favorite yoga corpse position afterwards. I barely had enough energy for the huge smile on my face.

During this short 30-day escrow period, I was impatient for my transition from LA resident to full-fledged desert dweller to be completed. My prediction that this would take eighteen months from start to finish looked plausible. It was a year-and-a-half since I had attended the manufactured home open house. Despite the fact that so many of my plans had been revised, delayed, rushed, cut back, and revised again, the conclusion was arriving right on schedule.

It is said that the course of true love rarely runs smooth. The same applies to going through escrow, an experience much like waiting inside a dark tunnel while stuck in traffic. You can see the light at the end, but have no control of when you'll get out. Having a good realtor to hold one's hand during this transition is an incredible help, and in that respect I was very fortunate.

There were so many papers to sign. I had to affix my signature to a huge pile of forms that promised things, some practical and some ridiculous. For example, I needed to affirm that there were no wild animals living underneath the house, no errant golf balls on the property, and no unsavory characters in the neighborhood. The animal and ball disclosures were easy to write off. But I fudged in not mentioning my irritating neighbor across the street.

Next was the inspection process. In an old house, there are many misalignments and decays an inspector can choose to make into mountains or molehills. I was lucky to escape with a modest cash allowance to avoid further repairs. A few more quick reconstructions were required before escrow could close.

In the final days of the eighteenth month of this relocating process, my realtor asked me to remove the last of my possessions and hand her the keys to the house. As much as I had been looking forward to leaving my former residence of twenty years and arriving at the end of this journey, I was overcome with a deep depression. After over a year of anticipation, it all seemed so sudden. I took a final walk through the home, retrieved a few items that I had inadvertently left behind, removed several keys from my key-ring, and then drove out of my now former neighborhood.

Shakespeare had it right when he wrote that parting is such sweet sorrow. Leaving the city of my birth and so much of my existence was a blend of agony and ecstasy. On that clear early autumn day, when I drove to what once was my desert getaway cabin, now a full-fledged house, my emotions were in a fog. But when I pulled into the driveway of my new residence, the inner clouds lifted. I knew I was finally home.

Under Construction - 2 New Rooms

3 rooms with the old patio

View from the patio

Re-slabbing for 2 new rooms

Framing over the new slab

Framing for the dining room

Framing for the bedroom

OSB & window in dining room

Closet/ sliding door in bedroom

Under Construction - Utility Room + Patio

Framing for the utility room

Slab for the new patio

Overhang for the new patio

New patio finished

Five-Room Haven

Living room in the 5-room house

Alcove open to four rooms

5-room house — exterior

View from the dining room

Part 6 – THE FOLLOWING YEAR
A Taxing Autumn

The months following my move out of the city I'd lived in for sixty years were not easy. Though grateful for selling my home in a difficult market, I was upset to see the economy get worse. My response to this was partly wise and partly fearful. I enrolled in a course to become a tax preparer, a field I was certain would be recession-proof. I found a class in my area that started right away.

I had to hop on the train immediately. That autumn I was immersed in the fine points of tax law and tables, studying hard and doing a lot of homework. After three months, I got my certificate and was offered a job as an entry level preparer at an office my teacher was setting up thirty miles away. The hours were flexible, so l could still do some part-time music teaching in L.A. Looking forward to this hedge against the bad economy, I was glad to be working when so many others were unemployed.

During the break between class and work, the weather went from fairly warm in November to incredibly cold in December. A 30-year storm of historic proportions visited the area. Within two days, we had over a foot of snow accompanied by power failures. At first, I enjoyed how my property became a winter wonderland. With my wood stove, I had no problem keeping warm. This was my first time being snowed in where I lived, a real novelty. But by the week's end, I was relieved to get my access to the world again. Fortunately, this happened before I had to start reporting to my new job.

The Winter Of My Discontent

The tax work turned out to be an assignment from hell. My teacher, who'd done a decent job of instruction, was a disorganized and inefficient employer. The new office had malfunctioning computers without clear instructions on how to operate them or how to process the customer forms. People started entering the office to get their returns done, and we employees had to learn on the fly. It was a stressful situation. He compounded the agony by complaining about every little mistake we made, when many of our problems were because of his mismanagement. All this work was paid at a rate barely over minimum wage, not to mention without any benefits.

Most of our clients had unrealistic expectations about taxes and tried to work schemes to bilk the government out of money. Their returns were not complicated, but the way they misrepresented themselves made the process more difficult. I was so disillusioned with this, by the time our hours were cut back and then reduced to zero I was relieved. If I was going to starve, I preferred to do it as an artist, not as a tax preparer.

The winter continued to be chilly and brutal. I caught a bad cold and had trouble throwing it off. Soon my part-time music lessons in Los Angeles dwindled down to a trickle. Everyone cut back on their discretionary spending, and music was the first thing to go. Turning on the TV magnified this gloom with reports of massive unemployment and people panicking about making ends meet. I hunkered down until spring and waited for signs of improvement.

The Green Shoots Of Spring

As the season began to change, so did my attitude. When the weather started warming, I put out some vegetable plants like I used to do in LA. Because this was my first experience living in the desert full-time, I didn't realize that more frosts were on their way and I would lose these seedlings when the cold weather returned. As the frosts became less frequent, I tried again, this time protecting my little plants with covers and taking some indoors.

In the back of my mind I'd been dreaming of planting fruit trees. Soon the local nurseries started getting truckloads of them. I did some Google research to see which were suitable for my area. The internet provided me with varietals, climate zones, and other invaluable information such as water and soil requirements, relative hardiness and maintenance needs. I discovered that some fruits like cherries and apples need cross-pollination from complimentary varieties that bloom during the same period.

One tree became two which became three and before I knew it, I had bought ten trees. I felt that as long as I was going to do this venture, I might as well spring for a tiny orchard. I had the space, time, and fortunately a virtually endless supply of water from my wonderful well.

The front of my property was soon lined with peach, cherry, and apple trees. On the north side of my house I planted an apricot, a plum and a fig tree, which all are self-pollinating. With each tree, I put up supporting stakes, administered the appropriate fertilizer and dug reservoirs around each plant to hold water. I worked hard, going to bed early, and rising early. I really enjoyed keeping farmer's hours, spending time every morning watering my trees, both new and old.

As my seedlings got bigger I transplanted some and bought others to put in large pots which I placed on shelves above what I hoped would be out of a rabbit's reach. Before long, I had tomato, pepper, and zucchini plants, as well as an herb garden, which included basil, oregano, dill and mint. By late summer, I had to shoo away a few pests and encircle my containers with chicken wire to insure that they were rabbit-proof. I used these vegetables and herbs often in my cooking. Everything was growing nicely.

Drip Irrigating Into Summer

I enjoyed watering my plants, but the task was sometimes daunting. I had 75 feet of heavy hose to drag around my property to several locations. A friend stopped by and encouraged me to put in a couple of new hose-bibs to make this easier. This seemed to be a good idea. I asked my contractor if he wanted a small job to help me do this. He suggested that a better idea would be to install drip irrigation. I was living on negative income and wasn't looking to spend more money. He assured me it would cost around $300.

It is always a good idea to double the cost of a job estimate. The price rose as supplies cost more than first thought. So did the labor. To stay close to my budget, I had to pitch in with some of the digging. We wound up lining PVC pipe and tiny sprinkler heads to about two-thirds of my plants with this system, leaving some areas remaining for me to water by hand. When we were done, this reduced my daily chores considerably. More importantly, because we put this all on a timer, I could now go away for a few days and have most of my plants and trees taken care of without me being there. During the hot summer months I was able to spend a fair amount of time camping in the mountains or near the beach.

In the middle of this irrigation project I received another desert initiation. After seven years of seeing no snakes on my property, I was surprised one day to find what looked like a rattlesnake in the utility room. While transporting my clothes from washer to dryer I looked down and saw something long, skinny, coiled and brown. To say I ran out of the room as fast as an Olympic sprinter is not an exaggeration. I called my neighbor, who is snake savvy, to help me out. He came right over and told me the creature was a harmless gopher snake that looked remarkably like a rattler, but wasn't. The reptile had come into my open room to partake of a rat inside. My neighbor took a simple stick and got the snake to wind around it, releasing the animal in the wash below my house. It sped away from us as fast as I had run from him. You can bet I've not left the door open to critters in that room since.

The drip system has been in place for a while. With regular controlled watering, my new and old plants have each responded beautifully. My fruit trees leafed nicely and I've harvested a few apples and figs. My main challenge has been keeping pests away from my vegetable garden containers. Besides rabbits, there are squirrels and other critters lurking around. This was a learning curve I was happy to take on.

Building and moving to my desert blog cabin has turned out to be a wise decision. I never could have predicted that a native-born Angeleno would feel so at home in this challenging environment. Life as an ex-pat desert dweller has had many more rewards than drawbacks. I spent almost two years crossing my own private wilderness to get to this promised land, and promising it is indeed. If anyone else has aspirations of doing something similar, I offer my heartfelt encouragement.

O magnet-South! O glistening, perfumed South! My South!
O quick mettle, rich blood, impulse, and love!
Good and evil! O all dear to me!
O dear to me my birththings all moving things,
And the trees where I was born
The grains, plants, rivers;
Dear to me my own slow sluggish rivers where they flow

Walt Whitman

The Following Year

Five-room house in the snow

Stella and snow in the backyard

Back yard finished

Ebenezer Von Kitty

Fruit trees and eucalyptus

Frontage road

*Author and Stella

*Author in his garden

•

• Photographs by Joseph Varga

• INDEX

ABOUT THE AUTHOR

Cat Cohen was born in the 1940s near downtown LA and called the City Of Angels home for six decades before resettling in the high desert above Palm Springs. As a child he played along the walk of stars on Hollywood Boulevard and rubbed shoulders with the entertainment world early on, making two guest appearances on Art Linkletter's House Party TV show. At the age of ten his family moved to the Jewish neighborhood near Canter's Deli on Fairfax Avenue where he learned to fish pickles out of a barrel and haggle prices at local bakeries. His adolescence was spent in the San Fernando Valley before attending UCLA where he majored in music.

While enrolling in graduate school in classical composition, Cat also played in a rock band six nights a week in Redondo Beach. After a stint in the Peace Corps in Micronesia, he lived in Santa Monica a block from the ocean. Here he taught piano and wrote songs and musicals, several of which were recorded, produced, and performed. For many years he taught songwriting at UCLA Extension. During the 1980s he was involved in the political and social movements of LA's gay, HIV, and recovery communities, work he continues in the Coachella Valley today.

An active member of the **Palm Springs Writers Guild**, Cat has ten self-published books on food, travel, music, and recovery. He is also a longtime **ASCAP** songwriter with pop, R&B, jazz and blues songs cut by recording artists **Cheryl Lynn**, **Syreeta**, **Freddie Hubbard**, and **Bo Diddley,** and has had his work featured in the **HBO** movie **The Rat Pack** and the **Universal** feature film **Undercover Brother**. Currently, Cat performs as a pop music therapist and leads sing-alongs in hospitals, senior homes, and rehab centers. . www.catcohenauthor.com www.catcohen.com www.amazon.com/CatCohen/e/B00GG0QB74

[Photo by Joe Varga]

www.ingramcontent.com/pod-product-compliance
Lightning Source LLC
Chambersburg PA
CBHW080518090426
42734CB00015B/3096